RFOK

D1195939

RFOK

MUSKOGEE
City and County

Sponsored by
The Five Civilized Tribes Museum
Western Heritage Books

MUSKOGEE   1982

MUSKOGEE
City and County

Odie B. Faulk

Senior Editor: C. W. "Dub" West
Business Biographies by Juanita Freeman

CONTENTS

Fern Mountain
MUSKOGEE OKLA.

Chapter One

LAND OF BEAUTY

In what now is east-central Oklahoma, three historic rivers—the Arkansas, the Verdigris, and the Grand—converge at a place known for years as the Three Forks area. This is the heart of Muskogee County, the reason why it was settled and the reason for its early prosperity. The Arkansas flows to this point from the west, a river born high in the Rocky Mountains from the melting snows of winter. Fed by a thousand tiny rivulets, it gathers strength as it flows down out of the mountains to meet the Great Plains, moving across Colorado into Kansas and then Oklahoma in stately fashion, curving and winding like some giant snake as the relentless pull of gravity creates its eternal desire to meet the sea. Because the soil of this region is soft and sandy, the Arkansas did not cut deep and jagged banks on the Great Plains.

As the river enters eastern Oklahoma, however, its banks became narrower and better defined, for the land is more resistant to erosion. This is a land of rolling hills and minor outcroppings of sandstone, at last coming to a region called the Prairie Plains. Comprising most of Muskogee County, this is an area of blackjack and post oak intermingled with mesquite and smaller shrubbery, a land of tall grasses, Indian paintbrushes, sunflowers, and honeysuckle. Wood bison, a smaller cousin of the buffalo, grazed this area, along with white-tailed deer, while squirrels chattered and fussed at them from the branches of the trees. Just to the east of the Three Forks area, in eastern Muskogee County, are the westernmost part of mountains known to geographers as the Interior Highlands. These are the western part of the Ozarks, that part usually called the Cookson Hills. Flowing out of this mountainous region of eastern Oklahoma from the north is the Verdigris, while from the northeast comes the Grand. The rainfall here is heavier, some 42 inches a year, and the two streams are lined with cottonwoods, giant live and white oaks, and pecan and walnut trees. At their point of juncture with the Arkansas, the rivers once were a mass of canebreaks. An officer of the United States Army in 1834 said this cane stretched "along the margin of the river, presenting an apparently impenetrable breastwork of dense green which extended beyond the reach of the eye. Its tall and slender stem reared itself in the air to a height of thirty or forty feet. . . . The stalks were so large and close together that our horses could not move forward without breaking through by main force."

Once joined, the three rivers continue as the Arkansas to the state that would bear the same name, eventually to blend its waters with the muddy current of the mighty Mississippi, all at last to flow into the Gulf of Mexico.

The exact date when humans first came to the Three Forks area is unknown, shrouded in the obscurity of unrecorded history. By the time of the first non-Indian exploration, the region was inhabited by the Wichita Indians, a confederation of the Taovaya, Tawakoni, Yscani, Waco, and Kichai tribes. Cousins of the Caddo of southeastern Oklahoma and northwestern Louisiana, the Wichita originally had lived in northern Oklahoma along the Arkansas River, but had fled southward when the Osages moved into that

Facing page: An example of the natural beauty in the area that would become Muskogee County, Fern Mountain is located four miles northwest of present Muskogee. Courtesy Five Civilized Tribes Museum.

area. The Wichita lived in permanent villages and, like the Caddo, had an economy based on hunting and farming.

The first Europeans to view the Three Forks area were French *coureurs du bois*—traders using the Arkansas River as a highway of commerce into the region. Bernard de la Harpe visited the area as early as 1719, finding an Indian village containing an estimated 10,000 people within a mile of the present Haskell. Soon other Frenchmen followed and guns, ammunition, knives, axes, beads, cloth, ribbon, and assorted other European goods were brought upriver by bearded, colorful voyageurs in pirogue and flatboat. These were traded for bales of mink, muskrat, beaver, and otter furs, even tanned buffalo robes, which made their way to New Orleans and eventually to France to be used to make milady's fashionable clothes. The French would leave behind place names that sing with the music of a distant culture: Poteau, San Bois, Fourche Maline, Verdigris, Salina, Cavanal, Salisaw, and Vian Creek (originally known as Bayou Viande).

The kaleidoscope of history turned in 1803 when representatives of the United States made the Louisiana Purchase in distant Paris. Soon American explorers were making their way up rivers which previously had been known only to sons of France. Simultaneous with this change of ownership of the land (in a European sense of the word), the Osage Indians moved in to displace the Wichita. In l802 the license granted Auguste Chouteau, a merchant living in St. Louis, had been revoked by the governor-general. Unwilling to lose this profitable trade, Auguste sent his half-brother Pierre to persuade the Osages to remove from their traditional homeland in Missouri to live along the banks of the Arkansas in what is now Oklahoma.

Among those chiefs who agreed to this move were Clermont and Pawhuska. After the American purchase of the Louisiana Territory, Pierre Chouteau, who was appointed Indian agent to the tribe, could not persuade the Osages to return to Missouri. Eventually the government decided all the Osages should be removed to what would become the Indian Territory, and this would be accomplished during the next two decades. Thus in January of 1807, when the first American trading party arrived at the Three Forks area, it was to find Osages living there.

This trading party was headed by James Bogy, who when moving upriver met a party of Army explorers coming down the Arkansas. This was the party of Lieutenant James B. Wilkinson, an offshoot of the famed expedition led by Zebulon M. Pike. At the Great Bend of the Arkansas River (in present Kansas), young Wilkinson became seriously ill, and he and six men were allowed to start down the Arkansas. During the late months of 1806 they struggled with ice and sandbars on the Arkansas until arriving at the Three Forks area on December 23. There they were treated hospitably at the Osage village of Chief Cashesegra. In January of 1807 they set out downriver, meeting James Bogy and his party moving upriver. Upon his return to Louisiana, Lieutenant Wilkinson would recommend that the United States government should "establish a

"Buffalo Hunt by Indians," by C. Wimar, 1861. From a post card at the Oklahoma Historical Society.

factory [trading post] or garrison of troops" at the juncture of the three rivers.

Bogy had secured a license to trade with the Osages, loaded a boat with trade goods, and started upriver with a dozen men to man the oars. Arriving at the Three Forks area, Bogy ascended the Verdigris a short distance, erected log cabins, and began trading for pelts. Despite being caught up in fights between tribes contending for mastery of the area, Bogy stayed, and it was to his post in 1819 that famed naturalist Thomas Nuttall of Harvard College came in his travels of exploration. While recuperating from a fever at Bogy's post, Nuttall astutely wrote, "If the confluence of the Verdigris, Arkansas and Grand rivers shall ever become of importance as a settlement, which the great and irresistible tide of western emigration promises, a town will probably be built here."

Bogy was joined at the Three Forks area in 1817 by Robert Mosby French and Samuel Rutherford, who established a small settlement "on the south bank of the Verdigris River at the lower falls." This was on the opposite side from what would become first the village of Okay, later renamed Coretta. In 1819 they sold their holdings to men named Bozier and Pryor.

The Osage Indians were among those living in the Three Forks area prior to the arrival of the Cherokees and Creeks. This is how a group of Osage Indians were depicted during their visit to Europe in 1827 and 1828 under the guidance of Colonel D. Dilaunay. Courtesy Archives/Manuscript Division, Oklahoma Historical Society.

The next major event in the Three Forks area was caused by the arrival of yet another tribe of Indians, the Cherokees. Part of the Five Civilized Tribes originally resident in the southern part of the United States, the Cherokees early in the 19th century were under increasing pressure to remove westward. By 1817 the Cherokees already had signed away parts of North Carolina, South Carolina, and Tennessee, but landhungry whites wanted more of their domain. That year Andrew Jackson negotiated another treaty with the tribe calling for it to give up yet more of its traditional homeland in return for land between the White and Arkansas rivers. According to this Treaty of 1817, migration to this new homeland in the west was to be voluntary.

The land to which the Cherokees were to remove was in the western part of what then was Arkansas Territory, but which eventually would become Oklahoma. In 1816 Major William Lovely, the Cherokee agent, had met with the Osages at the mouth of the Verdigris and obtained Osage agreement to a cession of land in east-central Oklahoma that included all of Muskogee County east of the Arkansas. The terms of this agreement were completed on September 28, 1818, when chiefs of the Osage Nation came to St. Louis and signed a treaty confirming what became known as "Lovely's Purchase."

By 1817 a number of Cherokees had voluntarily removed to Lovely's Purchase—only to meet with Osage resistance. When the newcomers began to arrive to settle there, the Osages reacted by taking to the warpath. There was open warfare with both sides conducting raids. The government responded by erecting a cordon of forts along the western edge of white settlement beginning with Fort Smith in 1817. The arrival there of Colonel Matthew Arbuckle in 1822 with companies of the Seventh Infantry brought a peace conference at Fort Smith that year at which both Cherokees and Osages agreed to an armistice.

A bowl recovered from the Spiro Mound by archaeologists. The mound builders had established a sophisticated culture in eastern Oklahoma long before the advent of recorded history in the region. Courtesy Archives/Manuscript Division, Oklahoma Historical Society.

Into this volatile situation also came raiders from the Choctaw Nation. Elements of this tribe, like the Cherokee, had been forced to remove westward from their original homeland in the South to make way for whites who coveted their lands, and they had to fight for a new place in the west. Moreover, the Arkansas Territorial Legislature wished to see the land involved in Lovely's Purchase opened to white settlement. When venturesome frontiersmen moved in, they soon were involved in quarrels and fights with the Indians already contending for the land.

Trying desperately to keep the peace between the various tribes were the licensed traders for whom war was bad for business. Among the traders who had settled at Three Forks were Captain

Barbour, a merchant from New Orleans who joined in partnership with George Brand. Because he was married to a Cherokee, Brand could reside legally in the area even before he joined with Barbour to secure a trader's license. Together they built almost a dozen cabins, cleared and planted some 30 acres, and even started a ferry service on the river. In 1823 they sold out to Auguste Pierre Chouteau, a member of the Chouteau family trading out of St. Louis with the Osages.

After purchasing the holdings of Barbour and Brand, Chouteau moved to the Three Forks area, leaving one of his lieutenants in charge at the Saline post. At Three Forks Chouteau soon had a staff of expert workers busily bundling bales of furs to be sent down-river on keelboats built in a shipyard he constructed. These were 50 to 80 feet long and capable of carrying 50 tons of freight. Once completed, they were loaded and sent downriver to New Orleans where the cargo was sold. Then the boat was knocked apart and the lumber likewise sold, for it was too difficult to pole these craft upriver.

"A Happy Plains Family at Home" as depicted by an artist in Century Magazine.

Chouteau was a man of such honesty that both Osages and Cherokees came to rely on him, as did the government when it negotiated with the tribes in that area. However, there continued to be skirmishes between the Cherokees and the Osages which Barbour and Brand and, after them, Chouteau could not halt.

Because of this friction, Colonel Arbuckle in 1822 recommended to his superiors in Washington that a garrison be placed at the mouth of the Verdigris River to keep the various tribes at peace and to stimulate white settlement in the region. Orders to this effect were issued early in 1824, and on April 9 Colonel Arbuckle left Fort Smith, marched his Seventh Infantrymen upriver, and on April 22 selected the location of Cantonment Gibson, named in honor of Colonel George Gibson, then Commissary General of Subsistence. Because there were several Indian villages and trading posts along the Verdigris, Arbuckle chose to locate the new post some two and one-half miles up the Grand River on the east bank. Supplies could be brought upriver by keelboats, poled upriver at the cost of many blisters and sweat, and in 1825 a wagon road would be surveyed to connect Gibson with Fort Smith.

Within days of their arrival at the new site, the enlisted men were put to work erecting breastworks and barracks. Unshaven and with long hair, they cut logs and quarried stone, they fought malarial and bilious fevers, ate the government's hardtack and bacon, scouted new territory, and—sometimes—fought Indian and white renegades, all for eight dollars a month. Little wonder that so many of them deserted whenever the first opportunity presented itself. Despite being undermanned most of the time, the soldiers completed the construction of the post by 1828.

The fort they built was some 250 yards from a wide ledge of shelving rock on the east bank of the river where boats could land. Enclosed by a 10-foot-high stockade measuring 222 by 238 feet were 39 one-story log buildings, 10 two-story buildings, two log blockhouses with two field pieces in each, a stone powder house (magazine), and a dug well. These provided quarters for officers and enlisted men, even for a bakery and library.

The building of what became known as Fort Gibson did much to stimulate steam navigation of the Arkansas to the Three Forks area. Within a month the *Florence* departed Little Rock bound for Fort Gibson carrying 30 tons of freight and recruits for the Seventh Infantry. The following year the *Spartan* and the *Louisville* likewise made this run, and thereafter steamboats regularly plied the waters of the Arkansas to bring supplies not only for the troops but also for the merchants and traders gathering in the vicinity.

The major difficulty these steamboats faced in coming upriver from Fort Smith to the Three Forks area was at what came to be known as Webbers Falls. There a ridge of argillite, a hard black rock, had not been eroded by running water across the years, leaving a drop of some three feet during times of low water and as much as eight feet in high water. A man known only as Thornton located there sometime during the 1820s to tow early steamboats over this riffle by a rope pulled by oxen, a service for which he received five dollars. His services were most in demand during the months when the waters of the Arkansas usually were lowest: January, February, and March. By the late 1820s the steamboats he helped tow not only brought supplies to Fort Gibson, but also were loaded with an additional cargo: Creeks forced to leave their home in Georgia in exchange for land in Oklahoma.

Facing page: Washington Irvin depicted hunting wood buffalo. Courtesy Archives/Manuscript Division, Oklahoma Historical Society.

Chapter Two

THE INDIANS ARRIVE

Along the Gulf Coastal region at the time Columbus arrived in the New World was a large and powerful group of Indian people known as the Muscogee, a word which has been translated as "People of the Holly Leaf Confederacy." They usually were called "Creeks" because they lived in a land of many streams. Comprised of some 50 to 80 villages and numbering some 11,000 to 24,000 individuals, they were called Creeks by the first Englishmen with whom they came in contact. Among themselves they had a tribal tradition that they came from the west, from a chain of huge mountains which formed "the backbone of the world." Migrating toward the sunrise, they had crossed a great river and come at last to their eastern homeland.

To their north were the Cherokee, a nation which believed that its seven clans had migrated across a large body of water onto the North American continent, reaching a new homeland in what is now Tennessee, Georgia, and the Carolinas. Here they found a favorable climate and a rich soil, and they increased in numbers and reputation. Originally their capital (or peace) town of Echota was on the south bank of the Little Tennessee River, but later this was moved to a place called New Echota (near the present Calhoun, Georgia).

Along with the other members of what came to be known as the Five Civilized Tribes—the Choctaw, Chickasaw, and Seminole Nations—the Creeks and Cherokees were caught up in the imperial rivalries of Spain, France, and England. The newcomers from an Old World failed to respect the high level of civilization attained by these people. The European colonists learned from the Native Americans: the trails to be followed, the animals to be hunted, and

The hardships of the "Trail of Tears" as depicted by noted Indian artist Dick West, who for years taught at Bacone College. Courtesy Oklahoma Historical Society.

the crops that would grow in the soil of that region. The Europeans courted the chiefs of the Five Civilized Tribes, wanting them as allies in their interminable wars but not appreciating their culture or respecting their rights. Then, when they grew more numerous, these newcomers would contend with the Indians for the land, wanting to kill off the Native Americans or force them farther west.

Christian missionaries began working among the Cherokee and Creek Nations as early as 1800, and in the next three decades many prominent tribal members accepted this faith. Moreover, these nations wanted their children educated, and schools were established. Several members of both tribes were college graduates. In their land of gentle mountains and broad streams, the Creeks and Cherokees were hunters and farmers, a few in each nation acquiring slaves and becoming Southern planters. George Guess, better known by his Cherokee name of Sequoyah, invented his syllabary in 1821, and a newspaper in the Cherokee language began publication in 1828. In short, the Creeks and Cherokees by the mid-1820s had a civilization similar in most respects to what white Americans claimed to want the Indians to adopt.

Yet in Georgia, Alabama, Mississippi, and Tennessee, there were whites who, casting covetous eyes on the acres cleared and planted by the Indians, easily convinced themselves that the Native Americans had no economic or political rights. Unable to drive the Indians from their land by force, they entreated the government at both the state and national level to remove these first owners of the land to some point distant in the west. When sufficient numbers of white voters demanded this removal, politicians listened.

It was John Calhoun of South Carolina who proposed a solution. While serving as Secretary of War in the administration of President James Monroe, he read the reports of Lieutenant Zebulon M. Pike's exploration of 1806-1807 and of Major Stephen H. Long's epic trek of 1820. Both soldiers had commented that the plains country constituted a "Great American Desert" forever unfit for people depending upon agriculture for subsistence. Secretary of War Calhoun concluded that this area therefore was the place to which the Indians from east of the Mississippi River should be removed—one big reservation in the west. President Monroe concurred, and on January, 27, 1825, recommended this plan to Congress, which likewise agreed. This became the first official Indian policy of the United States government, and Southern governors moved rapidly to implement it.

That same year of 1825 the Osage were induced to cede more of their land in Oklahoma to make way for those tribes being forced out of Georgia, Alabama, Mississippi, Tennessee, and the Carolinas. Represented by Chiefs Clermont and Pawhuska, the Osages agreed to give up all their remaining land in what would become the Indian Territory except for a 50-mile-wide strip running along the southern border of present Kansas from the 95th to the 100th meridian. This opened the way for the removal of the Five Civilized Tribes to that area.

The Creeks were the first to feel the pressure to move. Already they had been stripped of part of their domain along the Coosa and Tallapoosa rivers because of their pro-British activities during the war of 1812, and another 15 million acres had been taken from them in 1818. These two losses caused a majority of the tribe to oppose any further cessions—even to oppose talks that might lead to cessions. In 1824 the will of the majority was demonstrated by a tribal order decreeing the death penalty for any Creek who proposed selling land to the whites.

However, there were Creek tribal members who were willing to move west. This faction was led by William McIntosh, a mixed-blood related to the governor of Georgia. McIntosh believed the Creeks would prosper only when removed from white influences and pressures. When the United States government again approached the tribe about selling some of its land, McIntosh and his followers indicated a willingness to negotiate, and the Treaty of Indian Springs was signed on February 12, 1825. This provided for the cession of all Creek lands in Georgia and eastern Alabama in return for land between the Arkansas and Canadian rivers in the Indian Territory, along with a cash bonus of $400,000.

Although the Treaty of Indian Springs was signed only by McIntosh and 50 other Creeks, the government was so desperate for some means to remove the Creeks from Georgia that it chose to recognize this as binding and sent it to the Senate for approval. Within a month the Senate had approved it, causing consternation in the Creek Council. It immediately sent a delegation to Washington to protest, while simultaneously ruling that McIntosh was guilty of treason and subject to the death penalty enacted in 1824. On April 30, 1825, a large group of warriors surrounded McIntosh's home. Everyone inside except McIntosh and another signer of the treaty were allowed to leave, after which the house was set fire; when the two men emerged, they were shot.

President John Quincy Adams did nullify the Treaty of Indian Springs, but the tide of public opinion was against the Creek Nation. Finally the tribal leaders realized that bloodshed was inevitable unless some new accord was reached. Therefore a tribal delegation went to Washington in the spring of 1826, and a new treaty was signed on April 26 that year. This stipulated that most Creek lands in Georgia were to be exchanged for a new home along the Canadian River plus an immediate cash settlement of $217,600 and an annual allotment of $20,000. Moreover, the government was to furnish transportation for the move westward. In addition, the McIntosh Creek, as that faction was called, was to be moved at government expense and to receive an additional $100,000.

The McIntosh Creeks were the only members of the tribe to move immediately. On May 13, 1826, Colonel David Brearley, who had served with the Seventh Infantry, was appointed the Indian agent to oversee the removal of the Creek Nation from Alabama. In 1827 he brought a small party of the McIntosh Creek faction to the Three Forks area, and they decided they wanted to settle near the

The Great Seal of the Creek, or "Muscogee," Nation. Note that it reflects the agricultural heritage of the tribe. Courtesy Archives/Manuscript Division, Oklahoma Historical Society.

mouth of the Verdigris. This site was on the river and thus accessible to steam transportation, but also it was near Fort Gibson and therefore afforded the Creeks some protection from still-belligerent Osage raiders. At that time Colonel Brearley purchased some of Auguste Chouteau's buildings to be used as the Creek Agency headquarters. Assisted by Chilly McIntosh, son of the slain chief, Brearley arrived at the new Agency in February of 1828 aboard the steamboat *Facility* with 780 men, women, and children. By 1830 more that 3000 Creeks were living at this site betwen the Verdigris and Grand rivers. The result was settlement in the area so dense as almost to constitute a small city, although it was not designated one. Letters posted there were marked "Western Creek Agency."

The Creeks still in Alabama agreed on March 24, 1832, to cede all their lands east of the Mississippi and to remove westward. Signed by chiefs Opothleyahola, William McGillivray, and Benjamin Marshal, this treaty called for the federal government to pay all costs of removal and subsistence for a year after the Creeks arrived in their new homeland. The result for the tribe was chaos as some members resisted removal, whites prematurely rushed onto their lands, and the government was slow in providing promised aid. In 1836 General Winfield Scott arrived in Alabama to arrest all remaining Creek, shackle them, and start them marching west to the Indian Territory. 14,609 Creeks made this trek of misery and death, 2495 of them registered as hostiles.

In the Indian Territory the two factions of the tribe were reunited near Fort Gibson—with resulting quarrels about the right of leadership. At last a conference was held with the blessing of General Matthew Arbuckle, commander at Fort Gibson. The Upper and Lower Creek, as the two factions were called, agreed to a united government under the leadership of Chief Roley McIntosh. However, each group maintained its principal chief who sat side by side at the meetings of the General Council, which convened in what now is McIntosh County. The legislature of the Creek Nation consisted of two houses, the upper one composed of "kings" representing the various towns, and the lower one composed of "warriors" representing the people.

The government, meanwhile, was having difficulties with the Arkansas Cherokees. In 1826 Congress threw open this area, guaranteed to the Indians as a homeland, to white settlement. Naturally the Cherokees were shocked and dismayed by this action, and they sent a delegation to Washington to protest. The result was a treaty signed on May 6, 1828. This provided for an exchange of Cherokee land in Arkansas for a new home of some 7 million acres in eastern Oklahoma. This same treaty defined the western boundary of Arkansas and gave the Cherokees in that territory 14 months to remove westward. This treaty contained one other noteworthy provision: it recognized the genius of Sequoyah, awarding him $500 and adding another $1000 so the Cherokees could acquire a printing press.

A majority of the Arkansas Cherokees did not want to move away from the improvements they had made on their lands, but

Colonel A. P. Chouteau. Courtesy Archives/Manuscript Division, Oklahoma Historical Society.

they saw little recourse and began packing. However, once in their new homeland, they found themselves in conflict with the Osages, but they continued to build homes, clear land, and plant crops. There they were joined by Sam Houston, an adopted member of the tribe. Resigning as governor of Tennessee in April of 1829, Houston moved to the Indian Territory, settling near Fort Gibson just to the northwest, opened Wigwam Neosho, a trading post, and married Tiana (or Diana) Rogers, a Cherokee. Defeated for membership on the tribal council in 1831, he left for Texas in 1832, there to become a hero of the Texas Revolution and twice president of the Republic of Texas.

Another area of settlement was in the southern part of what became Muskogee County. Walter Webber, one of the chiefs of the Old Settler Cherokee, as they were called, moved in 1829 to the area of the falls on the Arkansas River, there taking the land from a white settler named Benjamin Murphy. The land at that point was excellent for farming, and a salt spring nearby early began producing that valuable commodity. Thus at that point grew a settlement known as Webbers Falls. A post office would be opened there on July 15, 1856.

While the Arkansas Cherokees were settling in the Indian Territory, their eastern kinsmen in Georgia were finding their lives increasingly difficult. Whites were steadily becoming more insistent that the Indians be removed westward, a pressure that became far greater when gold was discovered on Cherokee land. In 1829 the governor stunned the tribe when he announced that all Cherokee lands were the property of the state, an action with which Congress concurred on May 28, 1830, when it passed the Indian Removal Act.

The one ray of hope remaining to the Indians was the federal courts. Eventually the contest reached the Supreme Court in the case *Worcester v. Georgia*, with the court ruling in favor of the Cherokees in 1832. However, President Andrew Jackson refused to enforce the ruling, and the fate of the Cherokees and the other members of the Five Civilized Tribes was sealed.

One by one the tribes were made to accept the inevitable. The Choctaw negotiated the Treaty of Dancing Rabbit in September of 1830, accepting a new home along the banks of the Red River. Seminole chiefs signed an agreement with the government on March 23, 1833, calling for them to have a reservation between the forks of the Canadian River (taken from the Creek), but some Seminole resisted and a long, bloody war began in Florida. The Chickasaw signed their agreement of removal, known as the Treaty of Pontotoc Creek, on October 20, 1832, calling for a homeland inside the Choctaw preserve.

The leaders of the Cherokee Nation, guided by Principal Chief John Ross, resisted as long as possible. Ross, who assumed office in 1827, even journeyed to Washington in 1832 to fight removal. However, there were headmen willing to accept removal, leaders such as Major Ridge, John Ridge, and Elias Boudinot. Sensing a split in Cherokee unity, the government called for a general council

Washington Irving. Courtesy Archives/Manuscript Division, Oklahoma Historical Society.

to be held in December of 1835 at New Echota, Georgia. Officials of the Bureau of Indian Affairs arrested John Ross and held him prisoner during this conference to prevent his objections, and the result was the Treaty of New Echota. This called for a total cession of Cherokee lands in Georgia in return for $5 million and land in the Indian Territory.

John Ross, when freed, journeyed to Washington to protest the treaty, but the Senate accepted it and President Jackson signed it into law. The Ridge-Boudinot faction emigrated voluntarily under the terms of this agreement, but the Ross faction waited in Georgia and did nothing. Thereupon the government in 1836 sent General John E. Wool with troops to enforce the treaty. At bayonet point, Cherokee men, women, and children were horded into stockades and then marched westward. The task was completed in 1837-1838 by General Winfield Scott and 7000 soldiers. By trail and boat the Cherokees followed the *nuna dat suhn'yi* (Trail of Tears). Cholera and measles took a heavy toll in the fall and winter of 1838, as did cold weather—and heartbreak. Estimates of the death toll on this trek run as high as 4000—and included John Ross' wife.

In the Indian Territory there was no unity for the Cherokees, although a constitution was drafted in 1839 at a meeting held some 10 miles north of Fort Gibson at a place called Double Springs. There were three sharply divided factions: the Old Settlers (those who had moved from Arkansas prior to 1830), the Treaty Party (the Ridge-Boudinot faction), and the Ross party (which had endured the Trail of Tears). Feelings were so high that on June 22, 1839, the Ridges and Elias Boudinot were murdered, leaving leadership of that faction to young Stand Watie. Peace did not come to the tribe until a presidential commission came to the Indian Territory and negotiated what became known as the Treaty of 1846. The Cherokee seat of government was Tahlequah. There a two-house legislature enacted laws to be administered by the principal chief. Interpreting and judging these laws were a circuit court system and a supreme court.

Both the Creek and Cherokee people suffered horribly during their first months and even years in their new homeland. Fields had to be cleared and planted, a process that took time. These newcomers settled alongside streams, not understanding that western streams were frequently subject to flooding. Thus in their first years in the Territory they saw their homes washed away, their livestock drowned, and their crops ruined. These were the same years during which promised government rations either were not forthcoming or else were provided by some Indian Bureau officials so intent on cheating that much of what arrived was rotten. Moreover, the climate proved unhealthy to the newcomers, hundreds dying of "billious and intermittent fever" (malaria and typhoid).

Proud people accustomed to refinements of living were forced to endure in rude shelters, to subsist on whatever food could be gathered, and to work long hours to reestablish farms and homes. Such was their industry, however, that within a few short years they had transformed the area that would come to be Muskogee

County into a prosperous area and rebuild their way of life. Where once there had been only trees and prairie grass, there rose frame homes and even a few stately Southern plantation mansions.

The Three Forks area became a crossroads for much of the traffic to and through the Creek and Cherokee nations, for steamboats regularly plied the Arkansas River bringing supplies to Fort Gibson and to the licensed Indian traders residing in the territory. Moreover, Auguste P. Chouteau continued to operate his trading post, constructing keel boats which were sent down the Arkansas loaded with furs and agricultural produce. These boats, owing to the difficulty of getting them upriver, usually were sold at New Orleans for their lumber at a standard price of $3 per linear foot, so the process of building them was continuous.

Tullahassee Mission School. Courtesy Western History Collections, University of Oklahoma Library.

The Three Forks area also was the crossing point for the Texas Road, a wagon trail that entered what now is Oklahoma near its northeast corner, followed the Grand River down to Fort Gibson, crossed by ferry between the mouths of the Grand and Verdigris, angled to the south-southwest to Fort Washita, and crossed the Red River at Colbert's Ferry. Across this road traveled settlers bound for Stephen F. Austin's colony in the Mexican province of Texas. Traversing the road in both directions were Mexican merchants coming up from the south with a variety of trade goods and then returning with things wanted by darkeyed senoritas and mustachioed caballeros. Going down it were parties of hunters and traders, along with not a few adventurers simply wanting to see the other side of the horizon; months later they would come back with herds of horses, Spanish silver coins—and tales of strange sights and places. Along the Texas Road were unlicensed traders driving wagons loaded with whiskey illegally being brought to Muskogee County to be sold clandestinely to thirsty Creeks and Cherokee settlers. In the 1850s the Texas Road would be used by stagecoaches carrying passengers and mail, and it would be the scene of more than one holdup where robbers shouted some frontier equivalent of the old British highwayman's cry, "Stand and deliver."

Traveling down this same road or coming up by steamboat, but for a far different purpose, were missionaries hoping to win a harvest of souls for Christianity. In 1826 two competing organizations, the American Board of Commissioners of Foreign Missions and the United Foreign Missionary Society, united their efforts into one new body, the American Board of Commissioners for Foreign Missions. Their agents came to Christianize and educate the Creeks and Cherokees as well as to render medical assistance to them. For example, when the Creeks settled at the Three Forks area, the American Board assigned Abraham Redfield to serve the newcomers. In anticipation of his arrival in their midst, the Creeks built a two-room log schoolhouse measuring 30 x 16 feet. This was the first Creek school in the territory. Subsequently a mission, Ebenezer, would be opened, and in 1832 Isaac McCoy organized the Muskogee Baptist Church with six members at the Three Forks area.

Traveling either by river or Texas Road also were several distinguished visitors to the region. Thomas Nuttall, a professor at Harvard College and famed naturalist, came to the Three Forks area in 1819 and spent a month in the vicinity. Another noted visitor was Washington Irving, who came to the area in 1832 in company with a federal commission settling boundary disputes between the various tribes. He visited with General Arbuckle at Fort Gibson and with Sam Houston at his trading post before boarding the *Little Rock*, a steamer, which went down the Grand to the Arkansas, then up it to the Verdigris, and ascended the Verdigris to the Creek Agency. Irving, in *A Tour on the Prairie*, his written account of this journey, noted how beautiful was the region: " . . . the sandy banks of the Verdigris— beautifully embowered stream—gleam of sky along the water between the lines of trees which fringe each bank—moon rising among the groves." When the boat got underway the next morning, he reported:

> Verdigris river—beautiful dawn—while yet twilight pass a fire on the shore—Indians around it—canoes fastened close by. Streaming flights of wild ducks—pigeons in clouds, some rising from the sand bars where they go to drink and to pick up gravel; others flying in successive clouds over the trees—banks of river with growth of cottonwood—river of moderate breadth—finely wooded banks.

George Catlin, the noted artist, also visited the area. He came in 1834 in company with a troop of soldiers bound for the Comanche country. Catlin paused to paint several Indians whose faces intrigued him.

Helping these various pilgrims across the Arkansas River at the Three Forks area was a ferry operated by Chouteau's employees. This, along with Chouteau's trading post and many houses in the area, were swept away by the flood of 1833, perhaps the greatest in the history of the region. Even Fort Gibson was damaged by this inundation. Soon thereafter a fire swept away two houses at the Creek Agency, along with supplies intended for the Indians. The Agency was relocated on the bluffs overlooking the Arkansas (to the north of the present Muskogee), and there it would remain until 1851. The Baptist Church likewise moved there.

Floods again ravaged the Three Forks area in 1844, and occasionally there were grass fires which swept across the prairie from west to east when the grass became dry. Someone careless with a campfire or a pipe thoughtlessly emptied, even a bolt of lightning, lit a blaze that seemed to fly through the dry grass, both game and people fleeing before it in panic. And there were periodic outbreaks of many types of illness, especially cholera. At Fort Gibson, for example, 298 soldiers died in the years 1834 and 1835; in one

three-month period in 1835 alone, 600 soldiers reported themselves ill. One officer stationed there wrote that so many troops had died there of illness that the post was unofficially known as "the charnel house of the Army."

Pressure mounted on the Army to abandon the post during the 1830s in part because of the large number of soldiers who died there, but also because the buildings were deteriorating badly and the Cherokees were calling for its removal. However, General Arbuckle argued successfully that the installation should be retained. A bustling enclave, it had between 200 and 600 troops who went out to guard Santa Fe traders, preserve the peace between the various Indian tribes, and assist travelers on the Texas Road. To Fort Gibson on their way west came the uprooted tribes from the east, there to receive rations, farm implements, clothing, and other provisions. Thus after 1835 construction started on a new Fort Gibson, this one to be built of stone and located on higher ground. This site proved slightly healthier, for it was farther from the river bot-

The new arrivals in the Indian Territory built their homes out of readily available lumber and used some locally made bricks for chimneys. This home, built in 1823, was said to be the oldest house in the Indian Territory at the time the photo was taken. Located at Fort Gibson, it also supposedly was once the home of President Zachary Taylor. Courtesy Barbara Higbee Collection.

tom—and the breeding ground of myriad fevers. Construction on this post would continue until the completion of a barracks measuring 159 by 15 feet.

However, by this time the need for the post was declining, and the pressure to close it mounted steadily. Especially vocal in demanding that the post be closed were the Cherokees, to whom all buildings and the land would revert if it shut down. The Creeks protested that the fort should be maintained for their protection, but in 1857 the Army agreed and the soldiers were withdrawn. The Cherokee National Council thereupon established the town of Keetoowah at the old post site.

Another Creek complaint during this period was the Agency maintained for them. By the late 1840s the members of this Nation were unhappy that their Agency was too far removed from them, that they had to travel 30 or 40 miles across the prairie and make a dangerous crossing of the Arkansas River to get to it. The Agency was removed in 1851 to the south bank of the river just east of Fern Mountain (about three miles northwest of the present Muskogee). In the shadow of the Agency several merchants erected stores, and

Facing page: Missionary teachers at Tullahassee ca. 1878. Front row, left to right: Miss Nancy Thompson, Reverend and Mrs. William S. Robertson (parents of Alice Robertson), Augusta Robertson (sister of Alice Robertson). Back row, left to right: Miss S. Brown, Miss E. J. Baldwin, and Sammuel W. Robertson (Alice Robertson's brother). Courtesy Archives/Manuscript Division, Oklahoma Historical Society.

a small community grew there. Moreover, there was a school for Creek children at the Agency, although the children often were not regular in attendance.

By this time, the future Muskogee County was prosperous and peaceful. Life may have been threatened by nature and disease, but such had always been the history of mankind. To the residents of the area, theirs was a peaceful, placid existence growing steadily better. Schools and churches had been erected amid the farms and villages. Traders and boatmen regularly came to the Three Forks, there to meet with Creek and Cherokee trappers seeking to sell various types of peltries. The whistle of the steamboat regularly was heard on the river, coming upstream with manufactured goods and moving downstream carrying furs and agricultural products.

On arriving at their new homes in the Indian Territory, members of the Five Civilized Tribes found beautiful rivers and creeks in their new homeland, such as the Arkansas River shown here. Courtesy Archives/Manuscript Division, Oklahoma Historical Society.

By the 1850s Creek and Cherokee farmers, along with white tenants renting farmland in what now is Muskogee County, were raising far more than was needed locally; in 1846, for example, Creek farmers sold 1000 hogs to be driven to Illinois, and they exported 100,000 bushels of corn that year.

The Three Forks area thus was the commercial and business center of the Indian Territory. The arrival of a steamboat was a major event, for it brought passengers with news of the outside world, mail from business associates and loved ones, and merchandise ranging from brightly colored brocade cloth to perfumes and cologne water. Little did these people realize how their hard-won prosperity would be threatened—and changed—by the war clouds gathering over the Republic as men of reason in both North and South saw no recourse for their disagreement but sword and musket.

Facing page: George F. Pierce, D.D., a Bishop of the Methodist-Episcopal Church, South, passed through the Three Forks area in the mid-1850s and, in his book, Incidents of Western Travel, *wrote, "The country . . . is the most picturesque I ever saw. The views are sometimes enchanting. . . . Our Maker must delight in the beautiful or there would not have been such a seeming waste of tints and hues and all the forms of wild natural scenery." Courtesy Sara Jo Wilson.*

Confields such as this helped make the Creeks and Cherokees prosperous following their removal to the Indian Territory. Courtesy Oklahoma Historical Society.

Chapter Three

BROKEN DREAMS & BROKEN PROMISES

The rains of more than a hundred autumns have washed the blood from the land. The snows of more than a hundred winters have cooled passions that unleashed suffering and destruction in the Indian Territory, and the verdure of an equal number of springs has covered the scars of war. But the heat of more than a hundred summers has not cleared the miasma of rancor and hatred left by that most terrible of conflicts, civil war. Both the Creek and Cherokee Nations were caught up in the madness that swept across the United States between 1861 and 1865, and both suffered—and yet suffer—from their involvement in a quarrel not of their making.

As war clouds darkened the horizon of the republic in 1860, these two nations, along with the members of the other of the Five Civilized Tribes, found their position impossible. Slavery was traditional among them and was an established part of their agricultural production; thus their sympathies were Southern. However, it was Southerners who had evicted them from their traditional homelands.

On the other hand, the federal government was protecting them in their new homes, although newly elected President Abraham Lincoln held abolitionist views and had talked openly of allowing white settlement in the Indian Territory. Moreover, when the war began, the federal government withdrew its troops from all posts in the Indian Territory, thereby admitting it could not protect the Creeks and Cherokees from Confederate invasion. Lincoln and his advisors did not want the Indian Territory to be taken by the South, but defense of Eastern states apparently seemed more important.

John Ross moved slowly as agents for both North and South wooed the Cherokees. In April of 1861 President Jefferson Davis named Albert Pike of Arkansas as representative to treat with the Five Civilized Tribes. Pike, tall and broad-shouldered, was Massachusetts born and Harvard educated, but for almost three decades had been a newspaper editor and attorney at Little Rock, Arkansas. Enthusiastically he accepted the assignment, and soon he was in Tahlequah to meet with the Cherokees.

When an invitation came to join the Confederacy, old divisions in the Nation surfaced, as Ross had feared would happen. The pro-removal faction, led by Stand Watie, favored the South, while the anti-removal faction supported the Union and John Ross' leadership. Watie organized militia units with himself as commander and offered their services to Confederates in Arkansas, while Ross tried to adopt a position of neutrality. Again the Cherokees were a divided people—even after Cherokee leaders in October of 1861 signed a treaty of alliance with Pike in October.

With the Creeks, Pike's negotiations moved more rapidly. In July of 1861 they joined with the Confederacy, as did the Choctaws, Chickasaws, and Seminoles. All these agreements, including the one with the Cherokees, involved a Confederate recognition of the Indians' land titles. The tribes were to provide regiments for the South, one of Cherokees, a second of Creeks and Seminoles, and a third of Choctaws and Chickasaws. The Confederacy was to provide their equipment and pay, protect the Indian Territory from Union invasion, and deliver the annuities which the United States previously had paid the tribes. Under the terms of these treaties, the five tribes quickly raised 5000 soldiers, prominent among whom was Stand Watie who rose to the rank of brigadier general in the Confederate army.

The first battle in which these troops were used was against their fellow Indians. This campaign came because Opotheleyahola, a Creek headman, was unhappy with the treaty signed by his tribe with Pike. He had been absent while these negotiations had taken place, but his signature had been placed on the document. Upon his return he refused to recognize an alliance with the Confederacy, gathered those Creeks loyal to him, and retreated to a camp on the Deep Fork of the Canadian River. There they were joined by people from several other tribes— totaling some 6000 men, women, and children—and called themselves ''Neutral Indians.'' They intended to remain aloof from the conflict.

The Southern Cherokee Delegation to Washington D.C. in 1866. From left to right: Colonel John Rollin Ridge, Saladin Watie, Richard Fields, Elias C. Boudinot, and Colonel William Penn Adair. Courtesy Archives/Manuscript Division, Oklahoma Historical Society.

Unfortunately the pro-Confederates refused to let them live in neutrality. In November of 1861 Colonel Douglas Cooper, a former agent to the Choctaw, led a force of 1400 Indians and Texans against the neutrals. Opotheleyahola ordered his 6000 followers to begin an exodus toward Kansas. Cooper's scouts located them as they marched north, and a series of running battles were fought—at Round Mountain, Caving Banks (Chusto Talasah), and Chustenahlah. The neutrals fought for their families and their freedom of choice, and eventually they reached Kansas. On the way, however, hundreds died from bullets and from biting cold weather. And when they reached friendly forces in Kansas, many survivors had limbs amputated because of frostbite. Eventually some members of this neutral faction would return to the Indian Territory in Union uniforms.

While these sad events were unfolding, the war was brought home to what would become Muskogee County. Albert Pike, before departing for Richmond, decided that old Fort Gibson, be-

Map of the Three Forks area. Courtesy John W. Morris.

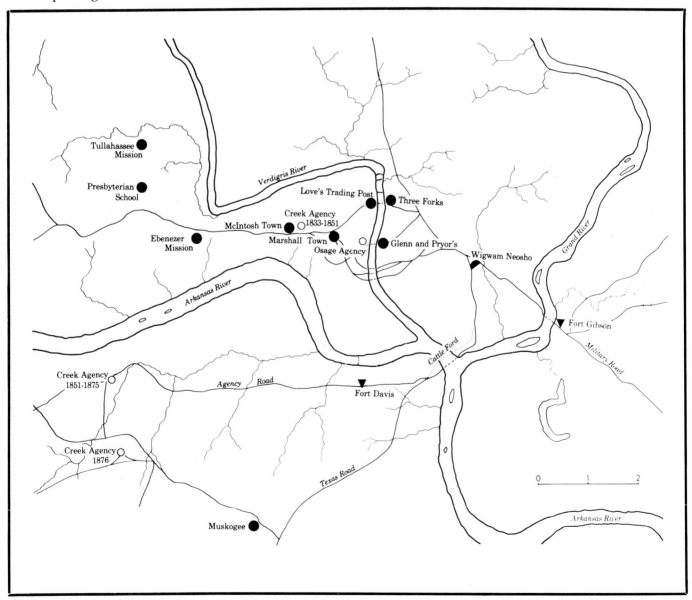

33

Opotheleyahola, leader of the Creek Indians loyal to the Union during the Civil War. This lithograph depicts him as he appeared in 1836. Courtesy Smithsonian Institution, Bureau of American Ethnology.

cause of its sad state of disrepair, was unsuitable as a headquarters for the Confederacy in the Indian Territory. He selected a new site on the south side of the Arkansas and some two miles south of the mouth of the Verdigris and ordered a new post built there. He chose this site because he felt the Arkansas would be an obstacle to invasion from the north and because the post would command the ford where the Texas Road crossed the river.

Built on a bluff by soldiers from Texas and Arkansas, as well as Indian troops, the post, named Fort Davis, had 13 log-and-plank buildings in a U-shape, the open end facing east. Two wells and a flagpole atop a 25-foot prehistoric burial mound completed the installation, which had no wall around it. Sentries posted on the east side had an open view of the Arkansas River, Fort Gibson, and the surrounding countryside. When General Pike returned in February of 1862, his command at Fort Davis consisted of the 1st Cherokee Mounted Rifles, led by Colonel John Drew; the 2nd Cherokee Mounted Rifles, commanded by Colonel Stand Watie; and a regiment of Creeks commanded by Colonel Daniel McIntosh. Pike hoped eventually to gather a force of 10,000 men at Fort Davis, but seldom did he have half that number.

In the spring of 1862 a Northern army commanded by General Samuel Curtis came out of Missouri to confront Confederates in Missouri, and Pike was ordered to move his Indian forces there to help Southern General Sterling Price defend that state. When he obeyed this order—in violation of what the Indians had been promised—he left the Indian Territory virtually undefended. On March 6-8 the Indian forces fought bravely and well in Arkansas at the Battle of Pea Ridge, Watie and his Cherokee troops capturing a Union artillery battery in what proved to be a Confederate defeat. Reports of the battle slighted the Cherokees' contribution, however, and Pike in anger withdrew to the southern part of the Indian Territory to establish Fort McCulloch. This left Colonel Douglas Cooper in command at Fort Davis.

Cooper's position never became secure, for he was poorly supplied and undermanned. Union officials recognized Cooper's weakness, and in April of 1862 they readied an "Indian Expedition" to regain control of the Indian Territory. This expedition consisted of troops from Kansas and other northern states along with Creek volunteers from Opotheleyahola's followers. Commanded by Colonel William Weer, this force set out on June 2 down the Grand River from Baxter Springs, Kansas.

Despite strong resistance by Watie and his Cherokee regiment, Weer won the Battle of Locust Grove, sent a column to occupy Fort Gibson, and managed to occupy Tahlequah without firing a shot. John Ross, captured at Tahlequah, was allowed to remove himself and his family to Philadelphia where he helped organize Unionists in the Indian Territory through his agents.

Weer's command did not take advantage of their victories, however, and in the summer of 1862 retreated to Kansas. Union planners thereupon began organizing another invasion in the fall of 1862, by which time the situation in the Indian Territory was one of chaos. Agents of John Ross were organizing the Indian Home Guard as a pro-Union force and spreading fear among Confederate Indians in the vicinity of the Verdigris River, and William Clark Quantrill arrived from Kansas in mid-1862 with his band of cut-throats, called irregulars, to wreak havoc.

In October of 1862 General James G. Blunt led a Union Column into the Territory, and Cooper retreated before him. This embol-dened the Ross faction of the Cherokee Nation openly to ally with the North, electing Thomas Pegg acting chief, reasserting that John Ross was the chief of the Nation, repudiating the treaty with the South, declaring Watie's government illegal, and freeing all slaves in the Nation. Thereafter, until the end of the war, there were two Cherokee governments vying for supremacy, the pro-Union Chero-kees having their seat of government at Fort Gibson from May of 1863 to the summer of 1865 and the pro-Confederate government operating from wherever Stand Watie had his headquarters.

To Fort Gibson came Indian and black refugees by the hundreds—and then thousands—seeking protection and food. Supplies came by wagon train which Watie and his Confederates sought to capture and divert to Southern use. The Arkansas River thus was a dividing line, Unionists to the north and Confederates to the south.

Stand Watie, the Cherokee General who fought valiantly for the Confederacy. The only Indian to hold a general's rank in the Confederate Army, Watie was the last Confederate General to surrender. Courtesy Archives/Manuscript Division, Oklahoma Historical Society.

On Christmas Day, 1862, Colonel William A. Phillips and the pro-Union 3rd Indian Regiment arrived at Fort Gibson, and two days later crossed the frozen Arkansas River to attack the Confederates at Fort Davis. The few Confederates there withdrew without firing a shot, and the victorious Unionists set fire to the buildings. Despite the cold, wet weather, the wooden buildings sent up a blaze that could be seen 25 miles away. The symbol of Southern control of the Indian Territory thus ended.

In July of 1863, Confederate Colonel Cooper, newly promoted to brigadier general, moved north to counteract the influence of the pro-Union Cherokee Home Guard. Meanwhile, Stand Watie, harassing the Yankees, attacked a supply train of 218 wagons at Cabin Creek only to be defeated and retreat to Honey Springs, a Confederate supply depot on the Texas Road south of Three Forks (near the present Oktaha). At this site in present Muskogee County, Watie and Cooper joined forces with the intention of rallying for an attack on Fort Gibson, which was seen as the key to the Union presence in the Indian Territory.

General Blunt came out from Fort Gibson to do battle before the Confederates could be strengthened from Arkansas, moving his troops across the river in boats below the mouth of the Grand. On July 17 the two sides fought. Heavy rains preceded this Battle of Honey Springs, and the Confederates had allowed their powder, already of inferior quality, to become damp—to their great disadvantage. Moreover, Blunt brought a large number of cannons with his troops. After a bitter and spirited battle, the Confederates withdrew.

At Webbers Falls, miles to the south, the local residents could hear the music of the cannon in the Battle of Honey Springs echoing off the hills, and they waited to learn the outcome. Too soon it came in the form of retreating Confederate soldiers, followed by

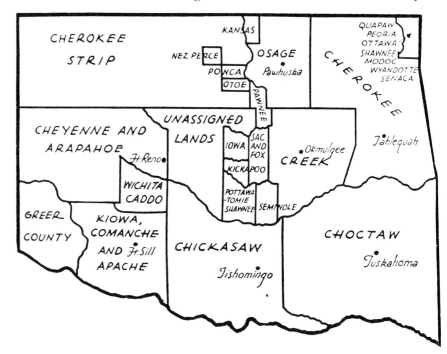

Union troops who burned Webbers Falls, forcing residents to flee with what they could carry.

In August Blunt likewise defeated General William Steele and a Confederate column marching into the Territory from Arkansas, and then on September 1 captured Fort Smith. This closed the upper Arkansas to Confederate traffic and signaled the end of organized war in the Indian Territory—but not an end to the suffering. Roving bands of thieves and killers, cloaking themselves behind the Confederate flag, spread terror in Muskogee County.

Stand Watie never let his men degenerate to this level, utilizing them in guerrilla raids and deep thrusts into Union territory. In 1864 he won notable victories at Cabin Creek and Pleasant Bluff, often distributing the supplies he captured among needy Indian refugees. For his brilliance and devotion to duty, Watie was promoted to the rank of brigadier general, but the cause he fought for was lost, and he surrendered on June 23, 1865—the last Confederate general to lay down his arms.

Not all Cherokees and Creeks had allied with the Confederacy during the war, but all would suffer during Reconstruction. Some Northern leaders intended not only to exact vengeance but also to destroy tribal government and nullify tribal ownership of lands. Most interested in breaking up the reserves were Kansans, who wanted all the Indians within their borders relocated to the south. In 1862 Senators Samuel Pomeroy and James Lane of Kansas had proposed that all treaties with the Five Civilized Tribes be voided so that part of their lands could be used for the resettlement of Kansas Indians. Congress agreed with this plan in 1863, and this became the basic plan of reconstruction for the Indian Territory.

Above: The homes of Creeks and Cherokees ranged from the large and elegant to the small and simple farm houses such as this one. Courtesy Archives/Manuscript Division, Oklahoma Historical Society. Left: The Creeks and Cherokees worked hard to rebuild their homes and renew their agricultural economies following the Civil War. Here a hog is being fattened with corn. Notice the large haystacks and farmhouse in the background. Courtesy Archives/ Manuscript Division, Oklahoma Historical Society.

Albert Pike in Masonic regalia. Courtesy Archives/Manuscript Division, Oklahoma Historical Society.

In September of 1865 Cherokee and Creek leaders joined other Indian chiefs at Fort Smith to hear the government's plans. Heading the government's commission was Commissioner of Indian Affairs Dennis Cooley who, in his opening statement, rocked the chiefs by saying that by joining the Confederacy they had "lost all their rights to annuities and lands," that their treaties had been voided, and that tribal laws no longer were valid. Each tribe would have to negotiate a new treaty with the United States, free their slaves, and cede a portion of their lands for use by other tribes. The conference then adjourned to meet in Washington the following spring.

In the meeting in 1866 Commissioner Cooley again led the federal negotiators. The quarrelsome Cherokees sent two delegations, one headed by an ill John Ross and the other by Stand Watie. Likewise the Creek Nation sent two leaders, Chief Daniel N. McIntosh representing the Southern faction and Chief Oktahasars Harjo, or Sands, leading the Northern Creeks. This left the two Nations negotiating from a divided position of weakness, while the Americans were united in their desire to force the tribes to give up part of their land.

Sammuel Chocote, Chief of the Creek Nation during reconstruction. Courtesy Archives/Manuscript Division, Oklahoma Historical Society.

Under the Treaties of 1866, as they became known, Creek and Cherokee prerogatives were sharply reduced. Slavery was ended, and the freedmen had to be adopted as tribal citizens and given land. Both Nations had to agree that the railroads could build across their lands. But most crushing was the loss of a large portion of their tribal domain. The Creeks were forced to cede more than 3 million acres, for which they were paid 30 cents an acre. The Cherokees lost their land in Kansas, and their Outlet was to be held in trust by the government until sold to the highest bidder.

The Treaties of 1866 brought dramatic change to the two Nations. No longer were they masters of their own destiny, makers of their own laws, and owners of vast stretches of land. No longer were their constitutions their sole foundation of government. Now functionaries from the Bureau of Indian Affairs would have a large

In November of 1892 the Cherokees enacted a law requiring citizens of the Nation to obtain a written certificate of permission to hire white people. Apparently this was done to discourage as much as possible the entry of white people into the Indian Territory. This particular permit was granted to Robert Ross on March 15, 1898, and entitled him to hire a white man for one month from the date of its issue. Courtesy C. W. "Dub" West.

say in how their governments were run.

In addition, they faced social and economic chaos. The property which had been developed in Muskogee County between 1840 and 1861 was largely destroyed, and their slaves, a large part of their work force, were freed. In addition, what became Muskogee County was being ravaged by roving bands of outlaws. Indian police, who prior to the Civil War had maintained order and enforced the laws, went back to work, as did United States marshals and deputy marshals working out of the federal court at Fort Smith.

Settling the divisions within the Creek and Cherokee Nations proved more difficult than rebuilding farms and capturing outlaws, however. Old hatreds had been fanned by the war, and reconciliation came hard. John Ross had died unexpectedly on August 1, 1866, while negotiating in Washington, and the following year

A map of Creek Nation in 1870. Courtesy Oklahoma Historical Society.

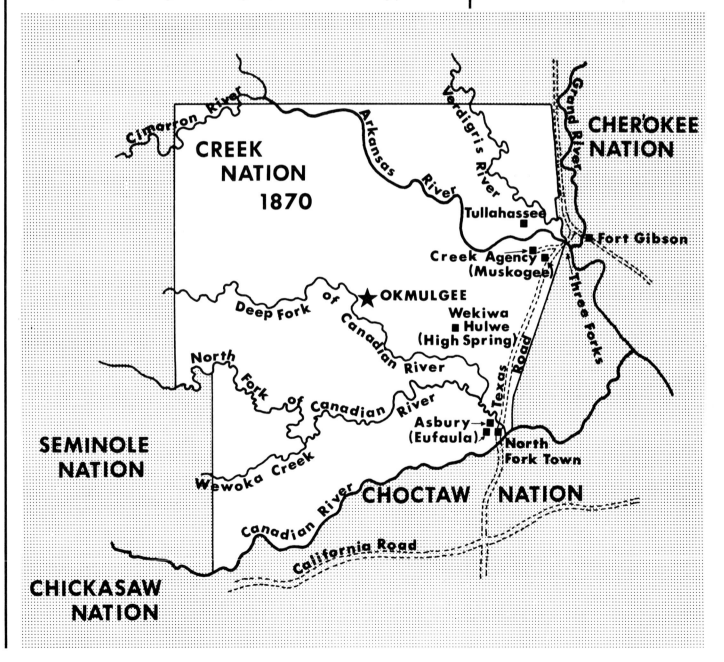

some of his followers joined with adherents of Stand Watie to form the Union Party. Thereafter this group controlled the tribe, and economic recovery then began.

The Creeks were unable to adjust so quickly. Samuel Checote, a Confederate veteran, was elected primary chief in 1867, but Union sympathizers within the tribe refused to accept him. This led to open warfare within the Nation in the early 1870s, and federal troops were required to restore order. For more than two decades thereafter, only the presence of soldiers prevented continued violence. With such quarrels openly evident, it was difficult for the tribe to return to prosperity. However, a new constitution, adopted

Colonel Douglas H. Cooper. Courtesy Archives/Manuscript Division, Oklahoma Historical Society.

in 1867, did allow Chief Checote and other tribal leaders to effect progress. Under this organ of government, the tribal reserve was divided into six judicial districts with a Supreme Court (which eventually sat at Muskogee) providing an ultimate decision for disputes. The Creeks were a hardworking and ambitious people, and by 1880 their fields again were green and thousands of horses and cattle grazed their pastures.

By this time dramatic changes had come to the County, changes that included the founding of a new city of promise, one that would grow to great importance in the Territory—and in the state which succeeded it.

Stickball was one of the favorite games of Creeks and Cherokees, and it could be quite rough when played by men. Here the women are playing the game. Courtesy Archives/Manuscript Division, Oklahoma Historical Society.

Chapter Four

BIRTH OF A CITY

When Stand Watie at last surrendered his sword and echoes of gunfire ceased to reverberate across the land, the soldiers at Fort Gibson cheered and shouted—and then returned to their monotonous duties of repairing the post, drilling, tending garrison gardens and livestock, cutting and hauling wood, and providing guard escorts along the Texas Road. Whenever possible the troops walked down to the small town that had developed to the south of the post. Also known as Fort Gibson, this settlement was frequently referred to by army officers as a "tough place." To it, one of them wrote, came "out-laws, fortune hunters and the riff-raff of all creation," especially on paydays at the fort when gamblers arrived in droves to separate the soldiers from their pay.

However, there was a genteel element in town, including the wives of army officers and merchants. Dances, literary readings, and religious services regularly were held in the town. For others there was the annual meet of the Fort Gibson Jockey Club, which had been founded in 1844 and which thereafter (except during the Civil War) sponsored races. Gentlemen took their ladies sailing on the Grand River or picnicking in the nearby mountains, and fishing parties went down to the river to see what might bite. Piano recitals and theatricals made Fort Gibson the social center of the Cherokee Nation during these years.

By 1871 officials in Washington saw no reason to continue the post's existence, and it was abandoned by all save a small detachment which operated it as a depot for the Quartermaster Corps. Yet such was the level of lawlessness in the Territory that the Cherokees wanted the post retained, and they argued that it should not be closed. Less than a year later the army sent a new detachment to occupy the post, the soldiers' task to end the illegal liquor trade and to "drive out the murderers and marauders." During the 1870s and 1880s, while U. S. Marshals from Fort Smith and Cherokee and Creek police tried to capture the lawless element attracted to the Indian Territory, the soldiers did their duty, fought boredom, and contributed to the building of a better society. Late in the summer of 1890 the post was abandoned again. Although reoccupied on brief occasions, its service had ended. However, a town of the same name, consisting of merchants and their families who had gathered near the fort, remained and would play an integral part in the affairs of the region.

Fort Davis, despite its brief existence of just a year, likewise became the location of a few businesses after the Civil War, for it was situated on the Texas Road near its crossing of the Arkansas and it had a landing (near the present Port of Muskogee). However, the settlement remained small, little more than a few shacks and a couple of stores.

A third area of settlement in what became Muskogee County was around the Creek Agency, which in 1851 had been relocated on the south side of the Arkansas River. The Bureau of Indian Affairs agent had brought his wife and children to live with him, and a few houses had been built there, including a Baptist Church. In 1867, J. A. Patterson had built a large log structure from which he

Facing page, top: Muskogee's main street as it appeared ca. 1889. Note the Phoenix Hotel and Restaurant in the left foreground. Courtesy Eileen R. Hewgley. Bottom: The celebration of the laying of the corner stone on the new United States Court House building, June 24, 1889. Courtesy Eileen R. Hewgley.

45

sold merchandise to Indians and blacks. J. S. Atkinson likewise set up shop in the shadow of the Agency building, as did several other merchants. Finally there was the small settlement of Tullahassee (in present Wagoner County), near which a Presbyterian mission and the Baptist Church were located. Across the rest of the County were scattered Creek or Cherokee Indians trying to eke a living out of the stubborn soil, except in the southernmost part of the county where Webbers Falls was reestablished in 1866 and where, for a time, Stand Watie would make his home. This small community gradually would grow because it had steamboat transportation and the soil around it grew bountiful crops. A chapter of the National Grange (a national farmers' group) would organize there in 1876, and a newspaper, the *Indian Sentinel*, would start there in 1890. A school had been opened there in 1853, but had been burned during the Civil War, as had the rest of the town. Another school opened there in 1878.

Alice Robertson, who long would be involved with events in the County, later would say, "Until the closing months of 1871 not a human habitation was in sight where Muskogee now stands. Only occasional wayfarers were seen traversing through the grass which led southward to North Fork and Fishertown or westward toward Okmulgee. Then many patient oxen dragged across the prairie great wagons laden with immense stone which were used in the bridge over the Arkansas."

This bridge was being built by the Missouri, Kansas and Texas Railroad, usually called the Katy. Under the terms of the Treaties of 1866, both the Cherokee and Creek Nations had to allow railroads to be built across their lands, and the Katy became the first to exercise this option. Slowly it crept across the Indian Territory, in large measure following the old Texas Road. At first railroad officials planned to run an extension from Gibson Station, as the depot west of Fort Gibson was named, to the post and then on to Fort Smith, Arkansas. However, the Cherokees stubbornly resisted this move, and the planned route was abandoned.

At the banks of the Arkansas the engines halted until the treacherous currents could be thwarted by a bridge. It took six months to span this river (at a point north of the present Muskogee). Huge wagons drawn by oxen brought timber and stone. When the 840-foot span was completed, people from miles around came to view it with wonder. From as far away as Fort Smith came steamboats filled with sightseers paying $10 each for an excursion ticket to come view the new structure.

On Christmas Day, 1871, the Katy sent its first engine, the "General Grant," across this bridge. Rails then were laid a short distance, and on New Year's Day of 1872 a station called Muscogee (as the name would be spelled until 1900) was established. The name Muscogee was selected to honor the Creek Nation. F. O. Martin, the locating engineer for the Katy, commented that a town consisting of "several tents and board shacks" sprang up the day after he drove his stakes. This location was about a mile north of the present downtown and in the shadow of old Fort Davis, and

Above: The Turner and Byrne Hardware Company Building as it appeared ca. 1889. The building was constructed in 1887. Courtesy Eileen R. Hewgley. Left: Clarence W. Turner, president of the Turner Hardware Company and one of Muskogee's pioneer merchants. Courtesy Muskogee, Indian Territory.

Joshua Ross, one of the pioneer merchants of Muskogee, opened his Red Front Store in 1872 at a corner that became Cherokee and Broadway. This portrait depicts Ross as he appeared in 1906, by which time he also was serving as a Notary Public. Courtesy Muskogee, Indian Territory.

there on January 8 a post office was opened with James L. Barnes as postmaster.

Alice Robertson later recalled, "At this first location, . . . Muscogee's first mercantile firm came into existence, the firm being composed of J. S. Atkinson and A. W. Robb. The two partners had a store at Gibson Station which they moved, transferring not only the stock of merchandise, but tearing down and putting up again the building which contained the goods, for in those days lumber was a costly commodity." A few weeks later the Katy chose to relocate at the present site of Muskogee because of the uneven character of the ground where the station first was built. Again Atkinson and Robb tore down their building, moved the lumber, and re-erected their store—the first building in Muskogee. Robb's private residence was the town's first house. Also moving to the new site was merchant J. A. Patterson.

A few days later Joshua Ross arrived to build and open his Red Front Store at a corner that became Cherokee and Broadway. Otto Zufall, who always recalled proudly that he was a "charter resident" of Muskogee, later would recall that he helped haul lumber for the first office building in town. This belonged to Dr. George W. Cummings, who also opened a drug store. That same year he was joined by Dr. M. W. Williams, who had been practicing at the Creek Agency. Several of the merchants who had been at the Creek Agency likewise moved their goods to Muskogee to be nearer rail transportation, and soon the town boasted a growing population. The enterprising Otto Zufall, who had come to the area to haul the brick, stone, and timber used in building the railroad bridge, saw an opportunity to make money by becoming what he later called "the first water superintendent." He delivered water "for 50 cents a barrel from the creek and 75 cents for drinking water" from a spring.

Other business establishments soon opened. The first hotel was housed in a tent, then in a long tin shed, for a time with no floor, on the east side of the tracks. Its owner, Colonel Mitchell, often waited on his customers barefooted. John Porter opened a restaurant in a tent, and George Zufall started a blacksmithy. Stockyards were constructed and operated by Major Freeman, and "Old Bill Brown" opened a barber shop. There even was a school opened that first year; Retta Robb started a private school and operated it for two years in a "tiny box house" on the north side of the post office.

Clarence W. Turner, who visited the area late in 1872 and who would move there a decade later to become a prominent merchant, commented in 1921 that at the time of his first visit tents were in common use as homes and businesses, that almost all whites holding a trading license (and thus eligible to be in the Territory legally) were crowding in, settling up and down the railroad tracks to the consternation of railroad officials. Creek Agent F. S. Lyon reported to officials in Washington that whites illegally were in the area and that he had "issued and posted an order just before Muscogee Station was located forbidding those unlawfully in the Creek Nation to raise, construct, or build any tent, house, cabin, or other building or to reside or do business along the line of the railroad." His orders were largely ignored.

The infant Muscogee thus was a peculiar town in that it had few of the institutions normally associated with new communities on the American frontier. It was not incorporated so there was no police force in the normal sense. There were no county officials, hence no sheriff. And there was no Territorial government or law enforcement officials, for the Indian Territory never had been organized. Thus to Muscogee came many individuals of a shadowy character: outlaws from the states, whiskey peddlers operating illegally, gamblers, and fugitives of a diverse nature. The Creek and Cherokee Nations had their own police forces and courts, but these had no authority over whites, many of whom were in the area without authorization. Thus the town could be a rough place, as the superintendent of the Katy noted when he reported to his superiors that the railroad's warehouse at Muscogee employed "four watchmen and we are not safe, even then. This place at night is dangerous, as half-breeds and whites are drinking, gambling, and shooting all night long." What desperately was needed was a better class of people who, through moral force, would bring stability. Fortunately such people soon were attracted to the opportunities of the region.

Almost a year after the founding of the town, J. A. Foreman arrived to open a wind-powered grist mill. It proved so successful that he soon had to adapt it to a steam engine to keep up with the demand. In October of 1875 the *Indian Progress*, the first newspaper in the County, was founded by E. C. Boudinot, but in December it moved to Vinita. However, that same year of 1875 the *Indian Journal* was started in Muskogee, and it would remain there until 1887 when it was moved to Eufaula (making it the oldest newspaper in Muskogee County in continuous publication). Other evidences of culture followed. The first sermon in present Muskogee apparently was given by a Presbyterian minister, the Reverend Timothy Hill, who noted in his diary, "preached to a full school house." His text came from Acts 16:9: "Come over into Macedonia and help us."

A severe plague of grasshoppers came in 1874, stripping plants of their leaves and leaving everything in desolation. This slowed the growth of Muskogee somewhat, for prosperity in large measure depended on the success of farmers in the area. Muskogee might well have remained but one more obscure village alongside the tracks of the Katy Railroad but for a stroke of good fortune that occurred in 1875. That year on August 18, the Reverend J. S. Murrow, Worshipful Grand Master of the Masonic Order in the Indian Territory, laid the cornerstone of the new Union Indian Agency on what then was called Prospect Hill (then Agency Hill, and now Honor Heights). Present at the occasion were William P. Ross, retiring chief of the Cherokees, Colonel E. C. Boudinot of the Cherokees, and Chief Samuel Checote of the Creek Nation. Completed at a cost of $5435 on January 1, 1876, this was to be the seat of administration where all government business with the Five Civilized

Creek Chief Pleasant Porter posing in his Plains Indian regalia for a post card. These sold well to tourists who wanted their Indians to "look like Indians." Courtesy Barbara Higbee Collection.

Rockefeller Hall Bacone Indian University as it appeared in the late 1880s. Note the students and faculty on the porch and posing in the windows. Courtesy Eileen Rooney Hewgley.

Tribes would be conducted. Previously each Nation had its own Agency. Securing the Union Agency made Muskogee the unofficial capital of the Indian Territory, the place to which all tribal members had to journey to conduct business with the government, the place to which traders had to come to secure or renew licenses. The town's future was assured.

By 1878 the town's growth was such that there occasionally were voices raised asking that the Indian Territory be made a state. Whites especially were in favor of such a change, for they had no rights in the Territory unless they were married to an Indian, worked for the government or the railroad, or leased farmland from either the Creek or Cherokee Nation. However, nothing came of this effort.

By 1881 Muskogee could boast two churches (Presbyterian and Methodist), a newspaper (published by the Creek Nation), thriving businesses, and some beautiful homes. Annually an "Indian Fair" was held, attracting participants from most tribes in the Territory and visitors from states to the east and north. That year the Methodist Episcopal Church petitioned the Creek Nation for permission to open a college, to be called Harrell International Institute, with Dr. Theo F. Brewer as president. Named for the Reverend John Harrell, an early missionary among the Indians, the institution opened first in the Methodist Church, then moved into its own quarters on Okmulgee between B and C streets with Sam Checote,

50

Charles Harris, Joshua Ross, G. B. Hester, F. B. Severs, W. N. Martin, E. H. Lerblance, and W. W. Folsom as trustees.

Yet Muskogee County was not so tame that nothing exciting occurred—as the so-called "Green Peach War" of 1882-1883 showed. This evolved out of the continuing quarrel between southern and northern branches of the Creek Nation. At the head of some 150 armed and mounted men, Pleasant Porter, a former Confederate soldier and currently Superintendent of Creek schools, restored peace by August of 1883. Thereafter he was always called "General Porter."

The same year the Green Peach War started, the Mission Board of the Presbyterian Church authorized the opening of a mission in Muskogee. Three years later its name would be changed from "Presbyterian Mission" to "Minerva Home" and placed under the care of Alice Robertson, daughter of a prominent Presbyterian missionary to the Indian Territory. Thus began what would become Muskogee's second institution of higher learning, for in 1894 Minerva House would become Henry Kendall College.

And in 1882 Clarence W. Turner, who had visited Muskogee just months after its birth, arrived in town to take up permanent residence, later saying that when he moved to the city it had only five white families. He purchased the Atkinson Hardware Company and began doing business under his own name. Eventually the Turner Hardware Company would become the largest emporium in

The home of a Miss Ross in Fort Gibson, said to be the oldest residence in town when this picture was taken in 1917. Courtesy Archives/Manuscript Division, Oklahoma Historical Society.

51

the Indian Territory, and he would own another 26 businesses in the region, including mills at Wagoner and Claremore.

In 1883 A. M. Williams, a reporter for *Lippincott's Magazine,* visited Muskogee, a city making its living from the cattle trade (Texas cattle being driven to railhead there) and from trade with farmers and ranchers in the vicinity. In an article in February of 1884 he described what he entitled "An Indian Cattle Town":

> There is a street of wooden buildings, some of considerable size, but of the rudest construction. One would not be surprised to see the whole town hauled off on a train of flat-cars someday, and it hardly seemed more permanent. . . . But, as the tent of an Arab merchant of the desert might contain a bag of diamonds worth a king's ransom, or a bale of priceless silks of Semarcand, so it is not to be supposed that the contents of these stores are necessarily as poor as their exteriors.
>
> On the contrary, although kid gloves and laces do not form an extensive feature of their stock in trade, their contents often represent a more substantial value in cash than those of some magnificent establishments in eastern cities. Nor are grace and intelligence wanting in the wives and families of these mercantile adventurers, and sometimes as sharply contrasted evidences of refinement and fashion will be found in these temporary homes as in the officers quarters of a frontier post.

Williams' description apparently was correct, for another writer said of Muskogee in 1883 that it was a place of "mud puddles, straying animals, no sidewalks, no paved steets, [and] Indians peacefully dozing in the sun, wrapped in blankets. . . . " The writer of this commented that J. E. Turner, Captain Severs, and Robert L. Owen owned most of the land.

The names mentioned all were prominent in Muskogee's early history. J. E. Turner had arrived in 1880 to build one of the first gins in the Indian Territory. Frederick B. Severs had moved to the Indian Territory from Arkansas to teach school to Creek children and had fought in a Creek regiment under Sam Checote during the Civil War. In 1868 he opened a store at Okmulgee, then started a second store in Muskogee, to which he moved in 1884. At that time he purchased extensive holdings and expanded his store until it was one of the largest in town. Later he would develop an entire block and build the Severs Hotel.

Robert L. Owen moved permanently to Muskogee in 1885 when he was appointed to head the Union Agency. His mother was the daughter of Thomas Chisholm, Chief of the Western Cherokees, his father a Virginia planter. Holding an earned master's degree, the 29-year-old Owen had been teaching at the Cherokee Male Seminary at Tahlequah and practicing law on the side when named Indian Agent. In 1890 he would help found the First National Bank of Muskogee and, after statehood, become one of Oklahoma's first two United States Senators.

Another name which became prominent in Muskogee's development first was heard in town in 1884: H. B. Spaulding. Moving north from Sulphur Springs, Texas, Spaulding labored for a time as

Settlers arriving in Muskogee in the late 1880s. Courtesy Eileen R. Hewgley.

The jail at Fort Gibson as it appeared on June 30, 1900. Some enterprising soul had placed small signs on it advertising "Pearline for easy washing." Courtesy Archives/Manuscript Division, Oklahoma Historical Society.

Mrs. H. B. Spaulding
Courtesy Mrs. Jack Vaughan

H. B. Spaulding
Courtesy Mrs. Carl Cawthorn

a carpenter, then accepted employment with J. A. Patterson and Company. Eventually Spaulding operated the dry goods department for that firm, but he aspired to more. Entering the cattle business, he expanded rapidly, soon running as many as 16,000 head on 200 square miles of lease land. He then operated mercantile firms in partnership with W. S. Harsha in Muskogee and R. B. Hutchinson in Checotah.

At the same time that Robert L. Owen came to Muskogee, so did the Indian Baptist University, more commonly called The Indian University. This was the brainchild of Almon C. Bacone, a Baptist missionary working among the Cherokees at Tahlequah; he opened the institution in that city in 1880 but wanted a more central location. In 1881 he came before the Creek Tribal Council to ask that land be set aside for the institution. Chief Checote along with a Creek minister, the Reverend William McCombs, argued forcefully for the project, and it was approved.

From John D. Rockfeller Bacone secured $10,000, and with the money he built Rockefeller Hall on a hill northeast of Muskogee. In June of 1885 the faculty and student body moved from Tahlequah in wagons to this new site. Old "Rock" Hall would serve as classroom, dormitory, dining hall, teachers' quarters, chapel, and administration building. Gradually growing until statehood, The Indian University stood at the apex of a fine system of education practiced by the Five Civilized Tribes. Each Nation had its own male and female schools, and these fed students into The Indian University, which for many years was considered a separate town named Bacone. The institution would rename itself Bacone College in 1910.

The prosperity of Muskogee during this era came in part from wholesaling and retailing goods to local residents and to farmers in the vicinity, but in large measure the dollars circulating in town derived from the cattle trade. Almost immediately after the end of the Civil War, Texas drovers brought herds of longhorn cattle up the Texas Road to be shipped from Baxter Springs, Kansas, to markets in the east. After the railroad arrived, moving rivers of beef continued to flood up the road from Texas to loading pens at Muskogee. Sometimes it took hours for a single herd to be moved through town. Cowboys yelled and cracked their whips, the horns of the cattle clacked together, and their hooves pawed up tons of dust in dry weather or turned the streets into one great boggy morass in wet weather. Once the cattle were penned up in corrals at the railroad depot, their bawling protests could be heard all across town.

Frequently these cattle came up and were held on ranches in the vicinity to be fattened for market. By the early 1880s, cattlemen in the area had organized the Muskogee and Seminole Live Stock Association and held annual meetings to plan roundups, register brands, and halt rustling. A Fort Smith newspaper, commenting about the growth of this industry in the Indian Territory, noted that in the spring of 1892 alone some 215,000 head of livestock were unloaded from rail cars between Muskogee and Vinita. Samuel Sondheimer saw opportunity in one facet of the cattle business

The United States Post Office and the business establishment of "Payne the Clothier" share the same building in Muskogee in the late 1880s. Courtesy Eileen R. Hewgley.

overlooked by others—trading in cattle hides—and he prospered by buying and shipping these to Eastern markets. Ranching thus early became a mainstay of the County's economy, although pecans were shipped out by the ton. Farmers gathered these and brought them in at the rate of two cents a pound.

Similarly, Muskogee was the headquarters for freighters carrying goods from the railroad depot and warehouse to lesser towns in the surrounding area. The shouting of these teamsters and the cracking of their whips could be heard at all hours of day and night as yet another wagon was loaded with foodstuff, hardware, and dry goods and sent on its way. Muskogee also was a major stop on several stage lines. Connections could be had there for Fort Smith, as well as for Okmulgee, Wewoka, and other Indian Nation towns. Muskogee was growing, and almost everyone found reason for optimism about the future.

Then on March 27, 1887, came the disaster feared and dreaded in most frontier towns, a great fire which swept through the infant city and burned "every business and house" between Patterson and Company's store and the Severs property. Refugees stayed in the Presbyterian Church until shelter could be found for them. As one survivor noted, however, the fire proved a blessing in disguise because merchants and homeowners "built back better." J. A. Patterson erected a two-story "skyscraper" at Main and Broadway, while C. W. Turner built a brick structure across the street. The town's newspaper, the *Indian Journal*, likewise burned. Its owners, Dr. Leo E. Bennett and Frank Hubbard, looked at the ruins of their property and decided to rebuild. When Hubbard asked Clarence Turner for an appropriate name for the new publication, he responded, "Why not call it the *Phoenix*? Let it rise from the ashes of the past."

With the rebuilding came a new respectability. Fraternal lodges, such as the Knights of the Pythias and the Masons, erected structures in 1888, while the Women's Christian Temperance Union, led by Mrs. Laura Harsha, crusaded that nothing stronger than beer be sold in Muskogee. Then in 1889 came news that a new federal court would come to Muskogee thanks to the lobbying effort of

A session of court in Muskogee. Although the exact date of the photograph is not known, it likely was taken between 1890-1896 because flags containing 43 stars were in use during that period. Courtesy Archives/Manuscript Division, Oklahoma Historical Society.

Pleasant Porter. Previously the nearest such court was at Fort Smith, Arkansas. The first session was held on April 1, 1889, in rooms of the new Masonic Lodge Hall with Judge J. M. Shackleford presiding; his particular duty was to protect the rights of Indians in the Territory.

Muskogee was growing, changing, uplifting itself into respectability. The census of 1890 showed it contained 1200 people—and yet more evidences of civilization. For example, that year the newspaper was advertising for agents to sell and install telephones, for a local exchange had opened. In fact, the first commercial telephone line in what would come to be Oklahoma had been installed to run from Muskogee to Fort Gibson by Ed Hicks, a Cherokee lad from Tahlequah. It proved such a success that it paid for itself in just six months. Muskogeeans began installing the instruments, and lines were strung through town, generally using the same poles on which electric lines were hung. The telephone exchange in Muskogee was in Clarence Turner's Hardware store. Turner likewise proved his willingness to adapt to other advances when he installed an ice plant and pioneered in the electrification of Muskogee.

And banking in a formal sense arrived in 1890, an outgrowth of

The newly completed United States Courthouse as it appeared ca. 1890. Courtesy Eileen R. Hewgley.

a service first provided by J. A. Patterson. At his store Patterson had a safe, and in it cattlemen early began depositing the large sums of money they handled. One day in 1879 Patterson was astonished to discover that he had $30,000 in his safe, prompting him to buy a larger and more secure strongbox. By the mid-1880s he was holding as much as $90,000 and performing such banking functions as issuing checks. Gladly he turned over such functions to the First National Bank, which secured a federal charter (the first in the Indian Territory) on August 1, 1890, and opened for business that year on August 22. President of this new institution was Robert L. Owen, who also was on the Board of Directors; other Muskogeeans on that board included A. W. Robb, F. B. Severs, C. W.

St. Joseph's College. Courtesy Barbara Higbee Collection.

Turner, P. J. Byrne, and T. B. Needles.

About this same time, John Henry Dill opened what would become another major bank in Muskogee. Arriving in Muskogee in 1889, he worked briefly for Clarence W. Turner, then began selling sewing machines. A thrifty man, he soon found himself with $700 surplus capital, and this he began loaning at interest. Realizing he was making more money from interest than from selling sewing machines—and deciding he would like to become a banker—he rented a storeroom on the east side of Main Street between Okmulgee and Broadway, bought some fixtures, and hung out a sign proclaiming the Commercial Bank.

Members of the Creek and Cherokee Nations, seeing the influx of unauthorized whites into their territory to settle at towns along the railroad tracks, naturally were alarmed and concerned—and well they might be, for Congress was debating the future of the Indian Territory during these years. Out of this debate would come legislation with far-reaching consequences for all the Indian nations, as well as for what would become Muskogee County.

The Agency Building in 1920 when it resembled a French Chateau. A tea room was downstairs and dances were held upstairs. Located on Agency Hill near Muskogee, the structure ultimately would become the home of the Five Civilized Tribes Museum. Courtesy Barbara Higbee Collection.

The Southwest Bottling Company of Muskogee located on Times Street between Okmulgee and Elgin in 1906. Courtesy Muskogee, Indian Territory.

Chapter Five

STATE CAPITAL OR COUNTY SEAT

Facing page: An architect's rendering of the proposed state capitol at Muskogee. Courtesy Muskogee, Indian Territory.

The Treaties of 1866 had forced the Creeks and Cherokees to cede much of the lands guaranteed them when they had removed from their original homes in the Southeastern part of the United States. Onto some of these ceded lands in the Indian Territory, the government had moved various nations of Indians from all parts of the United States. No whites were to be allowed into the region, and under the watchful eye of agents the Indians were semi-masters of their own destiny. The Treaties of 1866 also had provided that the nations might unite to form a regularly organized territory similar to what had been done in other parts of the West, and under this provision delegates to an Intertribal Council met at Okmulgee in 1870 and annually thereafter until 1876 trying to work out details for a union of all the tribes. Nothing came of this effort, however. Thereafter the region was referred to as the "Indian Territory," but it was an unorganized territory with each tribe running its own affairs, aided by an agent, and all subject to supervision from the Union Agency in Muskogee when it was established in 1875.

By the early 1880s, there still was "Unassigned" land in the middle of this territory, and the acres set aside so the Cherokees could reach the plains to hunt, the so-called Cherokee Outlet, were being used only by ranchers who leased grazing rights from the tribe. Thousands of dispossessed whites in Kansas and Texas cast covetous eyes on these open areas and wanted to homestead there. Under the leadership of David L. Payne, these land-hungry whites—called "Boomers"—demanded that Congress open the Unassigned Lands and the Cherokee Outlet to settlement. Impatient with the political process, some of these Boomers illegally entered the Indian Territory only to be evicted by soldiers enforcing the treaty rights of the Indians.

The Senate Committee on Indian Affairs came to the Indian Territory in the spring of 1885 to take testimony regarding what should be done, arriving in Muskogee in May that year. Under Chairman Henry L. Dawes of Massachusetts, this committee heard Indian leaders bitterly denounce the opening of the region to white settlement. Ranchers, fearing the loss of their lease lands, likewise opposed the opening of the area, but favoring it were railroad officials and landless whites. Two years later Congress passed what became known as the Dawes Severalty Act. This was enacted in the belief that eventually the Indian Nations should be dissolved and their members integrated into the mainstream of American life. It provided for the gradual dissolution of tribal government by forcing individual heads of Indian families to take an allotment of 40 to 160 acres. The thousands of acres left over after this process was completed would then be available for homesteaders.

Then on April 22, 1889, the Unassigned Lands were opened to white settlement in a "run." In one afternoon towns such as Oklahoma City and Guthrie were "born grown," and tens of thousands of farms were established. Cherokee and Creek leaders realized that enforcement of the Dawes Act would lead to an end of their dominance in the Indian Territory, and they resisted the intent of

61

the Dawes Act to the best of their ability—to little avail. In 1893 the Cherokee Outlet was stripped from the tribe and thrown open to settlement by a run. The payment to the Cherokees for the Outlet was distributed at the abandoned Fort Gibson on July 23, 1895, at which time 10,000 people gathered there. One observer noted that 125 businesses sprang up that day in front of the old barracks, not all of which would leave after the funds had been disbursed—and spent.

The interior of Cobb Drug Store, located on North Main in Muskogee, as it appeared ca. 1890. Courtesy Eileen R. Hewgley.

In 1893 Congress authorized negotiations to begin with the tribes so that land allotments could be made. Chairing the commission which first operated out of Fort Gibson was Henry L. Dawes. The Indians resisted as long as they could, whereupon Congress in 1895 passed legislation authorizing a survey of tribal lands to begin. Then the following year came an act directing that a roll of each tribe be made—which would be preliminary to allotment. Anyone whose claim for enrollment was rejected was given the right of appeal in federal court, including the one at Muskogee.

Thousands of people, some part Indian, some with no Indian blood at all, crowded into the Indian Territory hoping to get enrolled and thereby reap the benefits due Native Americans. Indians themselves were bitter at forced allotments, at the activities of the Dawes Commission, and at the fraudulent claims being advanced. But the work of the Commission proceeded, even after Chairman Dawes became so ill that he was forced to resign. Tams Bixby, first temporary then permanent Chairman, moved the Commission to Muskogee, and the work continued. To Bixby fell much of the task of leadership during the next decade of tremendous change in the Indian Territory. Also coming to Muskogee with the Dawes Commission was Ed Buddruss, whose son would establish Acme Engineering, a firm that would gain a national reputation for its work in air conditioning seed storage houses.

At last the various tribes began to realize that the end of the old way of life was inevitable, and on September 27, 1897, a delegation of Creeks reached agreement with the United States commissioners on the subject of allotments. The Creek Council rejected this agreement, but everyone—Indian and white alike—realized it was only a matter of time before allotments began. Congress assured this

A "conflagration" on north Main Street in Muskogee on October 24, 1890, draws a crowd of on-lookers. Courtesy Eileen R. Hewgley.

with passage of the Curtis Act on June 28, 1898.

Among the first in the Creek Nation to accept allotments were the former slaves of the tribe. The Treaties of 1866 had provided that the Five Civilized Tribes had to accept the freedmen on their tribal rolls as members, and thus these freedmen were eligible for land allotments. Wherever possible the blacks tended to cluster their allotments together, and thus within the Indian Territory there were many all-black towns. This had happened previous to enrollment and allotment. One such all-black community, named Marshall Town, had been formed between the Arkansas and the Verdigris in the 1870s, and had been the site of some violence when Cherokees claimed that residents of Marshall Town were rustling cattle from Cherokee ranchers. At the time of allotment, an all-black settlement named Twine was formed in Muskogee County some eight miles west of the city of Muskogee. Named for W. H. Twine, it received a post office on March 28, 1902, then two and one-half years later changed its name to Taft (in honor of William Howard Taft, then Secretary of War and later president of the United States).

Another all-black town was Chase, established some eight miles southwest of Muskogee in 1903. A post office opened there

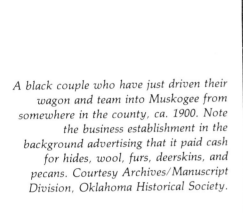

A black couple who have just driven their wagon and team into Muskogee from somewhere in the county, ca. 1900. Note the business establishment in the background advertising that it paid cash for hides, wool, furs, deerskins, and pecans. Courtesy Archives/Manuscript Division, Oklahoma Historical Society.

on April 9 that year. Five years later the name was changed to Beland, but the town never thrived as expected, and in 1926 it lost its designation as a post office. Yet another all-black town was Summit, so named because the location six miles southeast of Muskogee was the highest point on the Katy Railroad between the Arkansas and North Canadian rivers. A post office opened there on May 18, 1896, and would operate almost 20 years before closing.

Many whites, sensing opportunity, crowded into the territory, and Muskogee boomed during this period with dramatic growth. A new Baptist church was matched by the organization of Catholic, Episcopal, and Christian congregations. St. Mary's Hospital (later the Martha Robb Hospital), the first professional hospital in the Indian Territory, opened its doors in 1893. The Adams Hotel advertised in 1891 that it was "lighted with gas, heated with steam, electric enunciator [telephone], barber shop, bath and laundry in the house." A "real fire department" was organized, more schools were built, and a public library was opened. At every hand there was evidence of progress, and the *Phoenix* reflected the pride and optimism of its citizens when it proclaimed that Muskogee was "the best built town in the Territory, with the best hotels, an excellent fire department, with the most progressive citizens in Indian country, with the best allround climate in the world, the wealthiest town of its size in the southwest. . . . "

And still the growth and change continued. Clarence Turner

Engine House #1 of the Muskogee Fire Department in 1906. Notice the horsedrawn pumper unit. Courtesy Muskogee, Indian Territory.

opened an opera house to which came touring theatricals and musicals. Other theaters followed in the years ahead: the Hyde Park, the Wigwam, the Hinton, Convention Hall, the Broadway, and the Lyric. Names historic in the American theater trod the boards in Muskogee: Sarah Bernhardt, Otis Skinner, Madam Shumman-Heink, Madame Tetrazzini, Maud Powell, and Harry Lauder. Promoting such appearances was Grant Pauley, who made no money as a self-appointed impresario.

There likewise were advances in business and industry. J. A. Patterson, before his death in 1894, opened The Patterson Round Bale Gin and Compress to handle the increasing cotton crop of the County, while his Muskogee Roller Mill at the junction of Fondulac and Main streets was opened to grind flour. However, so little wheat was grown in the County that he concentrated on grinding cornmeal and feed. Bran and corn were shipped in by railroad car lots to be milled and then sold to ranchers and farmers in the region.

In addition to the regular sources of employment and income in the County—farming, ranching, merchandising, wholesaling, railroading, and steamboating—another industry, one more attuned to the somewhat distant future, made its appearance in the County in the mid-1890s. On September 19, 1895, the Creek Oil and Gas Company was incorporated by A. P. McKellop, Thomas J. Adams, and Taylor Chissoe, members of the Creek Nation, and J. M. Givens, L. J. Baker, and F. C. Hubbard of Muskogee. The new company began drilling a well near Severs' Gin (on the east side of the railroad tracks), and on October 30, 1896, at a depth of 1200 feet struck oil. However, there was no way to market the product, and the excitement subsided for several years.

Muskogeeans were so proud of what they were accomplishing that even another fire, this one on February 26, 1894, which consumed eight downtown buildings, did not diminish their positive feelings about their future, which they knew was destined to be great. Late that year they submitted a bill of incorporation for the city to the Creek Council, but it was rejected by Chief Pleasant Porter of the Creeks and the members of the Council. So certain were some citizens that incorporation and statehood would soon occur that in 1896 a seal was copyrighted boasting Muskogee as the "Star of the New State."

Yet there were continuing indications that the wild frontier days were not entirely gone. The hunting of "slow deer," as local citizens usually referred to wild hogs, was common almost at the outskirts of town. And robberies were far too common. The editor of the *Phoenix* was moved to comment on September 7, 1893, "You may kill off the Dalton and Starr gangs, but we will still have bank robbers." Apparently the editor's cynicism was justified, for in the summer of 1895 there were reports that the United States' Marshal's office was swamped with applicants wanting writs served on

Saint Mary's Sanitorium, established in 1893 by Dr. F. B. Fite, was Muskogee's — and perhaps Oklahoma's — first hospital. Courtesy C. W. "Dub" West.

horse thieves and other criminals hiding in the Nations. Several accounts survive of visits to Muskogee by Belle Starr, the Dalton Gang, the Cooks, the Cherokee Kid, and the Buck Gang. However, Muskogee's banks were not robbed, probably because they were so far from the edge of town.

Dr. Leo E. Bennett was appointed the U. S. Marshal for the Indian Territory in 1897, and his deputies kept the pressure on the outlaw element, and gradually this lawlessness would diminish. One of those helping in this process was James F. "Uncle Bud" Ledbetter, who came to the Indian Territory as a railroad detective, then in 1895 accepted employment as a Deputy U. S. Marshal. Later he would become city marshal of several Oklahoma towns, chief of police of Muskogee, and sheriff of Muskogee County.

As the end of the 19th century neared, Muskogeeans saw only good things ahead. The Thanksgiving issue of the *Muskogee Times* for 1897 noted that the city had 75 business houses, a mattress factory, three oil wells, an electric light plant, two mills for corn and an "expensive" one for flour, six churches (Presbyterian, Methodist, Baptist, Catholic, Episcopal, and Christian), more doctors and lawyers than towns twice its size, and five "flourishing" schools: Harrell Institute, The Indian University, Henry Kendall College, Nazareth Institute, and the W.C.T.U. school. And at nearby Fort Gibson was a different kind of school, one founded by a remarka-

Above: A "houseboat" on the Grand River near Fort Gibson, ca. 1900.

Above: The country side in Muskogee county still was bountiful in game in 1907 as these hunters in the Cookson Hills proved. Courtesy Sara Jo Wilson. Left: The aftermath of the great fire of February 23, 1898. Courtesy Leona Wipfli.

The notorious outlaw, Belle Starr, as she appeared in 1889. Courtesy Archives/Manuscript Division, Oklahoma Historical Society.

Leo Bennett, 1889. Courtesy Archives/Manuscript Division, Oklahoma Historical Society.

ble individual.

Laura A. Rowland arrived in Fort Gibson in 1897 and announced that she would open a school for the blind, for there was no such institution in the Indian Territory. Most people scoffed at the idea, for Laura Rowland herself was blind. With donated dollars, she opened the doors of this institution early in 1898 and soon had more than 50 students. Eventually she married William Lowery, a blind Cherokee, and the two continued the school with appropriations from the Cherokee and Chickasaw National Councils. After statehood the institution was renamed the Laura A. Lowery School for the Blind and received state appropriations.

What the Thanksgiving, 1897, issue of the *Phoenix* did not note were the drawbacks still to be overcome by those living in Muskogee at that time. A "Board of Trade," forerunner of the modern Chamber of Commerce, was formed late in 1896 to address the town's problems. On the Board of Directors of this organization were names prominent in Muskogee's early history: P. J. Byrne, A. W. Robb, John Adams, H. C. Warth, J. E. Turner, A. P. McKellop, W. T. Hutchings, Robert L. Owen, F. B. Fite, W. A. Maddin, F. B. Severs, H. B. Spaulding, F. C. Hubbard, and Clarence W. Turner. These people pointed out that Muskogee, because it had no legal standing in the Creek Nation, was without a charter and the usual town officials, such as police and courts.

Muskogee thus could not legally enact taxes for municipal improvements. The town, despite its location near the Arkansas River, had no source of pure drinking water; families still had to buy it from a man who delivered it by tank wagon at a cost of 25 cents a barrel. There was no way to finance the construction of city streets and sidewalks. Likewise, there was no sewage system, and every home had its outhouse out back. Most families still kept chickens and pigs along with a milk cow or two, and every home

A view of the growing town of Muskogee as it appeared from atop the Maddin Building in 1906. Note the numerous horses and carriages and the sign of the "Misfit Clothing Parlors." Courtesy Muskogee, Indian Territory.

had its stable for the horses used to pull the family buckboard or wagon.

Youngsters growing up on farms in the County worked alongside their parents, for farming then depended on human and animal power. The labor was intense and unremitting, and there were few diversions for children. The major crop in what would become Muskogee County was corn, with hay a distant second followed by wheat, cotton, and oats. For these farmers a trip to town was a major event, coming perhaps once a month and bringing memories to be recalled fondly during the days between. Schools were for the fortunate few; once youngsters learned to read, write, and do a little "figuring," many parents felt they had learned enough and kept them home to work on the farm.

In town, however, there was much to entertain youngsters. Louis W. Duncan, who moved to Muskogee in 1895 and who would have a distinguished career in banking in the city, recalls flying kites, spinning tops, shooting marbles, and having corn cob fights, but "Baseball was our main diversion." There was the annual visit of the circus to town, and there were the exploits of the local outlaw gangs to be discussed. On July 4 there would be a parade and speeches, along with fireworks and a big picnic dinner. On Halloween there were pranks and revelry, along with gorging on candy and fruit. Thanksgiving and Christmas were times for huge family gatherings, and attending church was an every-Sunday social as well as religious ritual.

Baseball was the sport for young men who wanted to entertain themselves on a spring or summer Saturday afternoon, for almost every company of any size had its amateur team. Young ladies gathered to cheer on the local "Casey" and provide the adulation that the young men craved. Older men boated and fished on the nearby rivers and hunted across field and forest in the surrounding

Robert L. Owen as he appeared in 1898. Courtesy Archives/Manuscript Division, Oklahoma Historical Society.

countryside. Proper ladies gathered for tea socials, discussed the latest novels from New York and London, and read poetry. And always there were social events; centered around the church, to mark the arrival of a new baby, and to note the impending nuptials of a young bride. Families gathered for huge reunions at picnics where tables were laden with food. There never was a dearth of something to do.

Suddenly in the spring of 1898 came news that electrified Muskogeeans. Federal Judges John R. Thomas and William M. Springer received telegrams on April 26 saying that the United States, which had just declared war on Spain, wanted 175 men from Muskogee and vicinity who could shoot and ride to join a mounted regiment of volunteers. The judges responded that Muskogee and vicinity could furnish 200 such men within a week and were authorized to begin mustering them. Judge Thomas, who locally became known as the "war governor" of the Indian Territory, began enrolling adventurous townsmen and cowboys from the countryside, and young boys watched goggle-eyed at the town parade ground as these "Rough Riders" drilled. The judge's son, John R. Thomas, Jr., was commissioned a lieutenant in one of the companies, and he would be wounded in Cuba. Another young son of Muskogee, Milo Hendrix, would be killed at San Juan Hill.

On May 16 these recruits entrained on the Katy for San Antonio where they joined the regiment headed by Colonel Leonard Wood and Lieutenant Colonel Teddy Roosevelt. Alice Robertson was at the depot giving out donuts and coffee to the soldiers, as she would whenever any troop train came through town. Muskogeeans then kept a close watch on the events of the Spanish-Amer-

An early combination barber shop and pool hall in Muskogee. Note the barber's chair in the foreground and the pool tables in the background. Courtesy Barbara Higbee Collection.

ican War, and proudly they cheered and paraded when their boys came home. The military spirit and pride generated during this war led to the formation of two militia companies (later incorporated into the Oklahoma National Guard).

The year 1898 proved dramatic for Muskogee in ways other than military. In February a petition bearing 240 signatures was filed in federal court asking for a decree incorporating the "town of Muskogee." On March 19 the petition was granted according to an attached plat, and townspeople at last began receiving legal titles and could feel secure in the ownership of the lots on which they had their homes and businesses. On June 1 that year an election was held in the same frame building where only weeks before the Rough Riders had been mustered into federal service. P. J. Byrne became the first Mayor. A month later came an announcement of the opening of the first public school, located on Second Street, with F. M. Butler as Superintendent. Shortly afterward came the formal organization of the Muskogee Fire Department, Charles S. Seekings serving as Fire Chief. And in September Henry Kendall College held exercises to mark its first graduates: Lucille Waldron, Benjamin McCurtain, and Norman Laird. These were the first college graduates in the Indian Territory.

One evidence of the increasing educational and cultural level of Muskogee and vicinity was the appearance in December of 1898 of the first issue of a new magazine, *Twin Territories: The Indian Magazine*, subscription cost one dollar a year or 10 cents an issue. The brainchild of 18-year-old Ora Eddleman, this was a sophisticated effort to show the world that Muskogee and the Indian Territory was not a wild frontier but rather a place of fine homes, cultured

Above: Charles N. Haskell, a railroad promoter and political leader for Muskogee who was elected Oklahoma's first governor. Courtesy Archives/Manuscript Division, Oklahoma Historical Society. Below: Wafuls Millinery Shop featured both childrens' and ladies furnishings. Courtesy Barbara Higbee Collection.

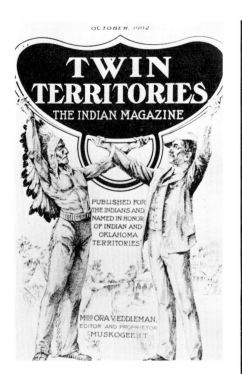

Ora Eddleman.

people, and stimulating literary endeavors. Its pages contained history, short stories, essays, and poetry by local authors and kept readers abreast of events in both the Indian and Oklahoma Territories. In addition to the many articles and stories which she personally wrote, Ora introduced into print such people as Alexander Posey, noted Creek poet, and she filled the magazine with excellent photographs and drawings. The remarkable Miss Eddleman, whose family published the *Muskogee Times*, made a financial and literary success of *Twin Territories* until her marriage in 1904 to Charles L. Reed, after which the magazine passed into other hands—and oblivion.

Just after the turn of the year 1899 came news important in the history of Muskogee County. On January 9 the Cherokee, accepted the provisions of the Dawes Commission, and exactly one month later so did the Creeks. Chitto Harjo, also known by the name Crazy Snake, would lead that faction of the Creek who did not want to take allotments, but the signing of these two agreements meant that soon there would be major political change in the Indian Territory. Harjo and his followers would arm themselves with Winchester rifles and resist for several years, but the old system was being forced out of existence.

As if to draw a line between the old and the new, much of downtown Muskogee was destroyed by a great fire on February 23, 1899. The blaze began about 5:30 a.m. at a cleaning plant on the east side of Second Street. Someone seeing the flames yelled "Fire" and fired a sixshooter, and the Fire Department responded immediately. However, a 60-mile-an-hour wind and zero-degree temperature, coupled with low water pressure, made the fight hopeless. The Fire Chief later would recall, "It was colder than blue blazes. It was so cold my boots froze to the tops. We were just one small department. . . . " Among the casualties were the Adams Hotel, the English Block, C. W. Turner's Hardware Store, the Katy freight depot, and the telegraph office. In fact, half the business buildings in town were destroyed.

The entire area was cordoned off with a rope, and disheartened owners of businesses sifted through the ruins to see what might be salvaged. Within days, businessmen and civic leaders gathered at Sondheimer and Sons' hide plant, on the corner of Second and Okmulgee streets, to discuss the future. No one dissented when a decision was made to rebuild. Like the Phoenix bird, they intended that their city "would rise from its ashes" bigger and better. In the days and weeks ahead, little could be heard in town except the rip of saws and the banging of hammers. The spirit of the town was shown in advertisements in the *Phoenix*. One of these was entitled, "Just 44 days after our Big Fire," and showed pictures of Turner's Hardware Store before and after the conflagration; the text stated that a giant sale would be held on $53,918.43 worth of merchandise which had arrived in "102 carloads" with "cash . . . paid on the spot, taking advantage of the discounts" so that customers could benefit from low prices.

As the year 1899 came to an end, the *Phoenix* put out a special

Chitto Harjo, or "Crazy Snake," leader of the Creek Indians who opposed allotment of tribal lands. Courtesy Oklahoma Historical Society.

Imprisoned followers of Chitto Harjo. Ironically, many of those who opposed allotment were placed on what was perceived to be the worst land. Later much of this land was found to overlay enormous pools of petroleum. Courtesy Oklahoma Historical Society.

The English Block, one of Muskogee's fine early buildings. At the time of this photograph the building housed, among others, the Oklahoma National Bank, the Muskogee Drug Company, and the Commercial National Bank. Courtesy Five Civilized Tribes Museum.

issue entitled "End of the Century," in which it discussed the history of Muskogee and vicinity. Among other notable events it recalled the visit of William Jennings Bryan to Muskogee in 1898, as well as that of Dwight L. Moody, the noted evangelist. The population of Muskogee was listed at 2000, and attendance at the five colleges and three public schools was 1200. Among these colleges was Spaulding Institue, which was the successor of Harrell International Institute. It was located in a remodeled building, the gift of H. B. Spaulding (a building later occupied by Muskogee General Hospital).

The first years of the new century brought many changes. Whites continued to flood into the County in anticipation of the allotment of land to the Indians, thereby freeing acres to be homesteaded by nontribal members. Ranchers who had been leasing vast tracts began seeking other pasturage as their old grazing plots fell to the plow. A reporter noted early in 1901 that there were 40 farms in the vicinity of Muskogee on what had been grazing land, and he predicted that the population of Muskogee would double during the decade. His estimate proved incorrect; the growth would astonish even the most optimistic: from 4254 in the census of 1900 to 14,418 in 1907.

By 1902 Muskogee was in a boom period, and everyone was talking about bigger and better times ahead. City sewage and

Second Street in Muskogee as it appeared in 1904. Courtesy Leona Wipfli.

waterworks systems were under construction, and there was constant talk of new railroads soon to be built. There was a boom in real estate prices, as evidenced by a quarter-page advertisement in the *Times* in July of 1902 proclaiming, "AN INVESTMENT IN MUSKOGEE DIRT IS LIKE GOLD DOLLARS OUT AT INTEREST. IT WORKS WHILE YOU SLEEP."

Early in 1903 one of the projected railroads became reality when the Ozark and Cherokee Central Railroad began service from Muskogee to Tahlequah. The principal promoter of this and two other railroads was Charles N. Haskell. A native of Ohio who had failed in his bid to be elected governor there, he arrived in Muskogee in 1901 with few dollars to his name but a widely recognized ability to raise money. By 1903 Muskogee could boast service by six railroads with 14 daily passenger trains and was a division headquarters for the Missouri Southern, the Katy, the Pullman Company, and the Muskogee Union. Haskell also would build an interurban line from Muskogee to Fort Gibson, giving connections with the Missouri Pacific Railroad, which had built to Muskogee's neighbor to the northeast.

As a result of land allotments to the Indians, the influx of new settlers, and the building of railroads, several small towns were born in the County during these years. On September 10, 1902, a post office opened at Boynton, a small community in southwestern

75

Cotton wagons waiting their turn at the gin in Muskogee, 1904. Courtesy Leona Wipfli.

A cotton compress at Muskogee. Note the railroad cars in the background waiting to ship the cotton. Courtesy Barbara Higbee Collection.

Muskogee County born because of the building of the Shawnee, Oklahoma and Missouri Coal and Railway Company. It was named for E. W. Boynton, the chief engineer of this road, and by 1903 it had a one-room schoolhouse operating. Three years later oil was discovered in the area (an extension of the Okmulgee Field), and the town briefly boomed; by 1904 there was a seven-room school-house.

Another railroad town in the County was Porum, although there had been two small settlements in the immediate area prior to the construction of the Midland Valley line. The original town there was settled about 1890 and called Porum Gap after the town's first postmaster, John Porum Davis, a prominent Cherokee. Two miles to the east of Porum Gap was the community of Starvilla, named for Frost Starr. In 1904 when the Midland Valley was con-

structing its tracks, both these communities moved, joining together to form a new town named Porum. It served ranchers in the area with banking facilities, stores, and a school.

In the far northwest portion of the County at approximately the same time the town of Sawokla (or Sawokli) was born. Originally settled by full-blood Creeks, it received a post office on June 17, 1902, and grew slowly until 1904 when oil was found nearby. Thereupon it was moved a short distance away and renamed Haskell (in honor of railroad promoter Charles N. Haskell). Far across the County to the east was the small community of Braggs. Originally called Patrick when a post office came there in 1886, its name was changed to honor Soloman Bragg, a local landowner. And in the southern arm of the County was Warner. Named Hereford when it received a post office in 1903 because of the Hereford cattle sales held there by rancher Campbell Russell, the townspeople chose in 1904 to rename their community Warner to honor Senator William Warner of Missouri. Other points of settlement in the

The Fite-Rowsey Building, home of the Dawes Commission in Muskogee. Located at Second and Okmulgee Streets, the building was erected in 1893 and also served for a time as headquarters for the Five Civilized Tribes. Courtesy Archives/Manuscript Division, Oklahoma Historical Society.

The original Dawes Commission. Front row left to right: M .W Kidd; H. L. Fellows, chairman; A. S. McKinnon. Back row, left to right: unidentified; Miss Anna Dawes, secretary; and Henderson M. Jacoway. Courtesy Archives/Manuscript Division, Oklahoma Historical Society.

County, usually where a school and perhaps a store had been built, included Yahola, Creekola, Council Hill, Beland, Summit, Wainwright, Keefeton, McLain, and Briartown.

By 1903 Muskogee, thanks to the growth of both city and County, had six banks with deposits totaling $1.2 million. Two daily and four weekly newspapers reported the growth of a town which could boast "a cotton compress, three cotton gins, two grist mills, [a cotton] oil mill, a vitrified brick plant, a concrete block plant, . . . 10 wholesale houses, and over 200 business establishments. Professional personnel numbered 50 lawyers, 20 doctors, 50 teachers, 10 preachers, and 100 stenographers. . . . The growing city had . . . organized fire and police departments, secured electricity and a long distance telephone exchange, and found it necessary to build new schools." The paving of principal downtown streets had begun with brick, and a few of the newfangled automobiles could be seen noisily making their way through town.

That same year came a renewal of drilling for oil in Muskogee County, and on December 3 a well was completed on the edge of town. A gusher, it sprayed oil across nearby houses. To process the crude flowing up from the ground, a refinery was completed in Muskogee in 1904, the first in what would come to be Oklahoma. In addition, a streetcar line was under construction and in 1905 would begin providing service to most parts of town. A spur also was run north to the Arkansas River where an amusement center, known as Hyde Park, was located.

Residential building matched commercial growth because the streetcar system made it possible for homes to be built farther from downtown. By this time Muskogee had homes that would have been an asset to any city in the nation. Because of all this spectacular growth, townspeople liked to refer to their city as "Magnificent Muskogee— Metropolis of Indian Territory," or, more eloquently, as "Queen City of the Southwest."

During the early years of the 20th century the political future of the Indian Territory was a topic of conversation almost everywhere people gathered in Muskogee. By this time most residents firmly believed that statehood for the Indian Territory was just around the corner and that their town would be the capital of the new state. Yet there were those who argued that the Indian Territory would be joined with the Oklahoma Territory to the west to form one state; this was referred to as Joint Statehood for what everyone called "the Twin Territories." Certainly there were sufficient people in the two areas to merit statehood, for the census of 1900 had shown 790,391 people in the Oklahoma and Indian territories.

In the Indian Territory there was little sentiment for joint statehood. Indian leaders feared that whites would dominate all offices in a single state government, and as early as 1902 they began to work to have the Indian Territory become the state of Sequoyah. Representatives of the Five Civilized Tribes met at Eufaula that year to form an executive committee to consider the various alternatives. Nothing came of this effort, however.

Yet such was the fear of joint statehood that in July of 1905,

78

without sanction from Congress, leaders of the Five Civilized Tribes and influential whites in the Indian Territory issued a call for the election of delegates to a constitutional convention. This met in Muskogee on August 21. white, red, and black residents of the Territory voted in the election of the 182 delegates. Presiding at this so-called Sequoyah Convention was Chief Pleasant Porter of the Creek Nation, with Alexander Posey, a noted Creek poet, serving as secretary. W. W. Hastings, a Cherokee, chaired the committee that drafted the proposed constitution, with Charles Haskell working quietly behind the scenes to achieve harmony.

The result was a document calling for formation of a state called Sequoyah with 48 counties, a two-house legislature, a supreme court and judicial system, and a state capital—to the astonishment of Muskogeeans—at Fort Gibson. On November 7, 1905, the voters of the Indian Territory ratified the Sequoyah constitution by a vote of 56,279 to 9073.

Unfortunately this document—and idea—found little favor in Washington. The President and leaders in Congress preferred single statehod, and on June 16, 1906, President Roosevelt signed an Enabling Act that authorized a constitutional convention for one state. This called for the election of 55 delegates from the Indian Territory, 55 from Oklahoma Territory, and two from the Osage Na-

The Muskogee Oil Field in 1906. Note the steam boilers used to power the cable tool rigs. Courtesy Muskogee, Indian Territory.

tion. Meeting at Guthrie, Oklahoma Territory, on November 20, with Charles Haskell serving as Democratic Party Whip, the convention completed its work on March 15, 1907. The voters subsequently ratified the new constitution, Congress accepted it, and President Roosevelt proclaimed the new state in existence on November 16, 1907, the 46th star in the national flag. In elections held that fall, Charles Haskell of Muskogee was elected the state's first governor, and Robert L. Owen was named one of Oklahoma's first United States Senators.

On statehood day in Muskogee, train whistles blew, bells rang, and fireworks exploded. But there was fear of domination from the western part of the state, especially on the part of the Indians whose special status had ended. Tams Bixby had closed the books of the Dawes Commission on June 30 that year, his work completed. In all Bixby, with modesty and efficiency, had overseen the distribution of 20 million acres to 100,000 allottees. Saloonkeepers were almost as unhappy at statehood as the Indians, for prohibition had been decreed by the voters in the same election that saw the constitution ratified.

80

Yet the overall mood in Muskogee was positive on statehood day despite the recent loss of Henry Kendall College to the upstart town of Tulsa (eventually the institution would be renamed the University of Tulsa). New oil wells had been discovered in the County, and some oilmen were saying that Muskogee would become the center of the state's oil industry. More than 500 private homes, along with a new convention center and courthouse, were under construction. Postmistress Alice Robertson could report that Muskogee's gains in postal receipts were the greatest in the state since 1900, increasing an astonishing 1088 percent.

Such was the optimism that town boosters had formed the "100,000 Club," an organization dedicated to increasing the city's population to that number. These boosters had such contagious enthusiasm for their city that in 1907 they were able to bring the Trans-Mississippi Congress to Muskogee, A. C. Trumbo and A. W. Patterson building a Convention Center in which this gathering was held. This did much to focus desirable attention on the city and to promote its growth in the immediate future.

Anything seemed possible in Oklahoma's second largest city as a new era dawned.

J. Paul Getty spudded in his first well on New Year's Day, 1916, in northern Muskogee County. On February 3 the well hit oil at a depth of about 1400 feet and produced approximately 700 barrels a day. Within a few months Getty sold his half-interest in the lease. Courtesy Cities Service Oil Company.

Chapter Six

THE BOOM CONTINUES

Facing page: The Griffin Grocery Company warehouse in Muskogee. Note the wagons being loaded with supplies for delivery to retail grocers. Courtesy Martha Watson Griffin.

Top: Muskogee Central High School Band, 1915. Back row, left to right: James Rogers, Mozel Montgomery, James Reid, Miss Ellen Russell (director), Boyd Lewis, John McFarland, Helen Johnson, and James Tisdel. Front row, left to right: Ellen Bramer, Naomi Scott, Jennie Anderson, Harry Gibson, Bertha Benedict, James Gibson, and Mary DeGraffenreed. Courtesy Five Civilized Tribes Museum.

Bottom: The Muskogee Country Club, shortly after the completion of the building. Courtesy Barbara Higbee Collection.

During the negotiations of the Treaties of 1866, Allen M. Wright, one of the Choctaw delegates, suggested that what had been known as the Indian Territory be renamed Oklahoma, a word derived from two Choctaw words, *okla*, meaning people, and *huma* (or *homa*), meaning red. The name Oklahoma, Wright suggested, would be appropriate, for this land would be the "home of the red man." In 1907 when joint statehood came, the area was named Oklahoma, but the Redman largely became a stepchild in the land named for him.

One of the first major changes with statehood was the introduction of public schools in every part of Muskogee County, as well as in all the area that had been the Indian Territory. The change to public schools, along with the end of tribal governments following allotment of land, meant the death of the system of education which both Creek and Cherokee nations had maintained. Another change which the new state effected in 1909 was creation of three colleges in eastern Oklahoma, among these Northeastern at Tahlequah, which was housed in the old Cherokee Female Seminary building.

The creation of this new system of public schools and colleges spelled disaster for Spaulding Institute, which died quietly in 1908, and for The Indian University. Almost overnight an institution dedicated to educating Indians and which had awarded many earned bachelor's and master's degrees ceased to offer any college work and was reduced to the status of a high school. Its students largely were residents of the orphanage maintained on the same grounds and named for the Reverend J. S. Murrow. Not until World War I would college-level courses be offered by The University, which was renamed Bacone College in honor of its founder. Thereafter Bacone would be a junior college with classes only at the freshman and sophomore level. Those who wanted a bachelor's degree would have to transfer elsewhere.

For residents of Muskogee itself, however, the first years following statehood seemed as golden as they had thought would be the case. The constitutional convention which had convened in Guthrie late in 1906 had drawn the boundaries of Muskogee County and had designated Muskogee the county seat. This led to the construction of a County courthouse, the election of County officials, and the addition of this payroll to the economy of the city.

Moreover, Congress on May 27, 1908, passed legislation that led to yet more allotments to Indians, thereby freeing tens of thousands of acres for sale. These acres then were added to the County's tax rolls, and they became home to farmers struggling to make a living on 160 acres. These farmers needed seed and implements, food, and clothing, most of which was retailed or wholesaled through Muskogee. The result was a spectacular growth in the County's population: from 37,467 in 1907 to 52,743 in 1910. The majority of these people were little more than the yeoman farmers envisioned by President Thomas Jefferson a century earlier: each family trying to raise or make almost everything it needed. To purchase those items that could not be raised or made, cotton increas-

Interior of the Beshara store at Haskell. Standing from left to right: Joe Beshara, Barney Dustin, Tony Beshara and Mrs. Dustin. Courtesy Marguerite Beshara.

ingly was raised in the County. Statistics in the census of 1910 show that corn was still the largest crop, but cotton was gaining fast and would have the most acres devoted to it by 1916.

This cotton was picked and hauled to market in the fall, and the cash received used to buy shoes and clothing, sugar and flour, and an occasional sack of candy for the children. Farm wives made their purchases from their butter and egg money, taking their surplus of these items to market in the County's small towns of Boynton, Braggs, Haskell, Oktaha, Taft, Porum, Warner, and Webbers Falls. With the exception of Warner and Taft, these communities did not benefit from statehood—and would be hurt by improved roads and the automobile which made access to Muskogee easier. Thus these small towns, with few exceptions, remained a place to buy groceries, go to the post office, get harness mended and horses shod, and send children to school. Warner was assured a future when Connors State College of Agriculture opened there in February of 1909. A junior college, its purpose was to upgrade farming in the region and to help ranchers by demonstrating the benefits to be derived from introduction of better bloodlines in local cattle. Taft benefitted from statehood when in 1909 the state located an institution for black orphans, along with deaf or blind blacks, in that all-black town. This provided a payroll from the state treasury which helped the local economy. S. Douglas Russell became superintendent of the institution, as well as editor of the Taft *Tribune*.

Fort Gibson would prosper during the first two decades follow-

The business district at Braggs. Courtesy Five Civilized Tribes Museum.

ing statehood, a period that some would call "the Golden Age" of the town. In 1911 it had 1374 residents, including six doctors, five attorneys, three gins, and was the market center for bumper crops of cotton, alfalfa, corn, and potatoes, along with cattle, hogs, and horses. However, it yet was largely a country town where, according to one visitor, loafers would sit on the wooden sidewalk in front of the stores, eat watermelons, and thow the rinds into the street where wandering bands of hogs would "grunt, squeal, fight over, and eventually devour them."

The town's citizens were interested in the fort for which their community was named, and efforts were made during this period to prevent it from falling totally into ruin. When the Army abandoned the post in 1890, the military reservation contained eight square miles. From this came the townsite of Fort Gibson, platted and surveyed in 1904. The Cherokee Nation, which inherited title to the property, sold these lots to individuals, as it did most of the old military stone buildings. However, that area around the old stockade was purchased by the town and given the name "Sam Houston Park." By 1923 the old post buildings were in a sad state of disrepair, and the Frank Gladd Post of the American Legion began a fund-raising effort across the state for funds with which to restore the post to its former condition. The effort, although unsuccessful, did focus attention on the historic significance of the fort, and gradually there would be an effort made to turn it into a state park.

The interurban trolley and the railroad provided the only connections with Muskogee for residents of Fort Gibson who wanted to shop in the big city, for there was no bridge across the Arkansas for wagons or cars. A ferry continued to operate across the river until businessmen in the two cities finally agreed privately to raise the necessary funds, and a bridge was completed in 1922 (it linked the two towns until the construction of a new span in 1969 so tall that river traffic could pass under it). The other major difficulty faced both by Fort Gibson and Muskogee in the two decades following statehood was the recurring problem of low water in the Arkansas which made river transportation increasingly difficult. Several people made gallant attempts to provide regular steamboat runs between Fort Gibson and Fort Smith, but increasingly this was difficult.

In Muskogee there also was a boom, the city almost doubling in population from 14,418 in 1907 to 25,278 just three years later. This meant Muskogee had grown by almost 21,000 people in just one decade and had matured from a small town into a metropolitan area. New business buildings were erected with dizzying speed, some of them even containing elevators. And construction of public works and buildings matched the business boom. In July of 1908 came a bond issue of $550,000 to be used in enlarging the waterworks and installing a storm drainage system in conjunction with the new street paving program. The following January the voters approved a $300,000 bond issue for school construction. In 1911 came approval of a bond issue of $390,000 for enlarging the water system and $175,000 for more schools. Residential construction likewise proceeded at a pace exceeding all forecasts, the newspaper noting in July of 1909 that 117 new homes were under construction

Broadway in Muskogee as it appeared in 1909. Note the Severs Block Building on the left, which by this time was home of the First National Bank. Courtesy Barbara Higbee Collection.

on the east side of town alone. One notable firm lured to Muskogee at this time was the Muskogee Iron Works, which the Commercial Club "landed" in 1909. This company would grow and expand, providing jobs for many city residents.

Everywhere it seemed there were evidences of progress: in the new three-story-plus basement Muskogee High School; in the construction of several "skyscrapers," including the Surety, Flynn-Ames, Carolina, and Barnes buildings; in the healthy operation of 10 banks in town; in the continuing discovery of oil and gas wells in the area; in the building of the largest power plant in the state by the Muskogee Gas and Electric Company (the predecessor of Oklahoma Gas and Electric Company); and in the construction of a Carnegie Public Library. In December of 1911 the Commercial Club (Chamber of Commerce) reported that Muskogee had 53 wholesale houses and 144 manufacturing plants. Also causing great optimism in the County at this time was a boom in oil production. Almost every booster advertisement for Muskogee noted the tremendous amounts of oil and gas being produced in the vicinity of the city, and local petroleum firms such as the Pure Oil Company's refinery were providing employment for a large number of people.

For reasons such as these, Muskogee, during the years immediately following statehood, liked to advertise that it had no unemployment and that its citizens, on average, were wealthier than residents elsewhere. One indication of the truth of this boast was the moving of the Town and Country Club from Fort Gibson, where it had been started, to Muskogee in 1909. A new golf course and clubhouse were laid out to the northeast of Bacone College by

A ferry on the Arkansas River between Creek and Muskogee counties. It was located seven miles east of Muskogee. Courtesy Five Civilized Tribes Museum.

*Right:
The Draughon's Business
College Baseball Team.
Almost every business of
any size sponsored
an amateur baseball team at
the turn of the century.
Courtesy Five Civilized
Tribes Museum.*

*Below: A view of Muskogee's
crowded Main Street.
Note the Turner Hotel on
the right, the Lenhart Theater
on the left, and the trolly
and its tracks. Courtesy
Barbara Higbee Collection.*

William Nichols, noted designer of fine golf courses. J. F. Darby, early-day oilman and entrepreneur, was elected president. Under his leadership and that of Tams Bixby, who succeeded him as president, the institution quickly grew in members and prestige. By the 1970s its excellence was such that it was chosen as the site of the LPGA (Ladies Professional Golf Association) national tournament. Playing in this meet was Muskogee's own Beth Stone, daughter of local newspaper publisher John Lewis Stone.

Another organization which would command prestige was the Rotary Club, which was organized when 30 men assembled on September 24, 1912, and elected Stanley Shelor president (this was the 87th Rotary Club in the world). A local Lions Club was organized in October of 1916 and soon was doing its part to better the community. And a fund-raising campaign, begun in 1914, culminated in the opening of a Young Men's Christian Association (Y.M.C.A) in the old Maddin Building in 1917.

Life during this period in Muskogee was exciting, for always there seemed to be some announcement of something newer, bigger, better. The six-day work week was common, but it seemed that most still had the energy to go to the Hinton Theater to see touring stage shows, magicians, and musicians. There also were fine parks to which families could go in the evenings and weekends. City officials had appointed a Board of Park Commissioners in May of 1909, and that November the city acquired 40 acres at Agency Hill from the Creek Nation for park purposes. Development began on what would become one of the nation's truly outstanding parks.

Trucks and employees of the Muskogee Wholesale Grocery Company. The trucks are loaded with products for distribution to retail grocery stores. Courtesy Blanche Baze.

William H. Taft campaigning in Muskogee in 1910. The city of Taft, located in the County, had been named in his honor. Courtesy LaVerne and Ritter Ray.

Boys still flew kites, played marbles, and cracked bat against baseball. They hung around the telegraph office to hear the results of each day's major league baseball play. They still gathered to stare in wonder when the circus came to town, and they gorged themselves sick every summer at what Muskogee liked to call the "State's Largest Free Fair," which continued the tradition of the International Indian Fair. Attempts were made on several occasions to get the state legislature to designate Muskogee's effort a "State Fair," which would have entitled the city to a $100,000 appropriation for upgrading the fairgrounds, but these efforts failed.

Young men rode the trolley to pick up their favorite ladies, each dressed in stiff, uncomfortable fashion, to picnic, to see theatricals or the new moving pictures, to go to church socials, to gather in someone's home to sing and play parlor games. Successful businessmen and their families took six-week summer holidays in Minnesota or Colorado to escape the heat, to swim and fish, to play bridge and golf, while others traveled to the Ozarks for the same reasons. During winter months, they took turns entertaining at

90

Celebrating the arrival of a new railroad in Webbers Falls. Courtesy Oklahoma Historical Society.

home, couples frequently dressing formally even for bridge games. Those without the funds for extended summer vacations and country club suppers did not envy those who did, for this was America where there was opportunity for all to rise. "Someday," the young man would mutter to himself—and work all the harder.

That world of ice cream socials, of quiet strolls in parks, of unbounded optimism in a greater future temporarily ended in April of 1917 when newspapers headlined America's declaration of war against Germany. Almost immediately recruiting offices in Muskogee were swamped by young men of the County anxious to serve their country. Many of these recruits were shipped to Fort Logan H. Roots in Arkansas. In August some 23 Muskogeans returned from this camp with commissions. Among them were Tams Bixby, Jr., and Julian B. Sanford, captains; the others received lieutenant's bars. Charles Ferguson was the first Muskogean reported to arrive in France; as a clerk on the staff of General John J. Pershing, he reached the scene of war on July 5. Many Creek and Cherokee lads trooped to colors, and they, like others from the County, would

Above: A regiment of the Nebraska National Guard from Lincoln, marching on Broadway Street in Muskogee on July 6, 1916. These troops apparently were on their way to serve with General Pershing in attempting to capture the Mexican outlaw Pancho Villa. Courtesy C. W. "Dub" West.

Members of the First Baptist Church of Haskell pose in front of the church building under construction. Note other church members working on the roof. The building was constructed in 1914. Courtesy Marguerite Beshara.

distinguish themselves. The Sixty-Sixth Engineers was organized in Oklahoma, Texas, Kansas, and Missouri, and many local boys chose to serve with that unit, which did its basic training in Maryland, then went to France. Louis W. Duncan, who served as a sergeant in this regiment, took time to write a letter home which described how Muskogeeans performed in this war: "To me it seems almost unbelievable that an army that only a few weeks ago were farmers, clerks, lawyers, etc., could come over here and make all of the armies of the world sit up and take notice; but that is just what they did. . . . " Muskogee County's roll of honor—those who died—would total 23, 14 of them from the town itself.

The war was strongly supported on the home front as those left behind sought to do their part. On July 4, 1917, the largest celebration of Independence Day in Muskogee's history was held, tens of thousands crowding into town to view the parade. The next day, July 5, was designated Registration Day. The Red Cross held a membership drive with a goal of signing up 5000 and raising $50,000, and young men registered for the draft. Alice Robertson, first by herself, then assisted by volunteers, met every troop train passing through town to serve coffee and donuts. Boy Scouts scoured the city and County to assist in Muskogee's first Liberty Bond sale, and Muskogee, which was assigned a quota of $800,000, subscribed $2,147,000. Families joined in observing "meatless Monday" and "wheatless Tuesday," agreeing with the slogan, "Food will win the war." Because almost everyone tried to do his part, all could join in celebrating when the newspaper on November 11, 1918, headlined, "WORLD WAR OVER."

The boys came home in the spring of 1919 to find some progress in the County. Roads gradually were being graveled or blacktopped; bridges, such as the one across the Canadian River, were being built over rivers and creeks to make the "Jefferson Highway" (later US 69) a reality; and automobiles were growing increasingly numerous as Henry Ford made the Model T affordable to almost every farmer. But the railroads were in growing difficulty, as evidenced by the sale of the Oklahoma Gulf line, whose first section had been built in 1902 by Charles Haskell and William Kinnefick to haul potatoes from the area around Fort Gibson.

Muskogee, both city and County, was being influenced by several currents sweeping the United States during this period. The great influenza epidemic of 1918 and the smallpox outbreak in the spring of 1919 tested and tried the health care delivery system of the city, causing doctors and nurses to work incredibly long hours. As these epidemics spread across the state, all churches, schools, and movies were ordered closed, and gatherings of more than 12 people were forbidden, even for funerals. Almost every family had at least one member sick, and business activity virtually ceased in Muskogee County.

One outgrowth of these pestilences was the opening of the Oklahoma Baptist Hospital on July 2, 1919, with hundreds of visitors swarming in to see "one of the southwest's most modern hos-

The Barnes Building, Muskogee. Courtesy Barbara Higbee Collection.

The Indianola Building, located at the northwest corner of Third and Broadway. It was also known as the Canadian Valley Building. Courtesy Barbara Higbee Collection.

pitals." Physicians and Surgeons Hospital (opened in 1914 and forerunner of Muskogee General) likewise did its part during these crises. Another addition to the health care facilities of the area came early in 1922 when it was announced that Muskogee would be the site of a $500,000 "Soldiers' Hospital" to be located "on the crest of Honor Heights." Projected as a state institution, it later would become a federal institution and renamed a Veterans' Hospital. Early in 1923 a new City Hospital opened adjacent to Soldiers' Hospital, but in 1926 it would be sold to the federal government to become part of the Veterans' Hospital.

Muskogee also became the home of the Oklahoma School for the Blind, as the Lowery School for the Blind was renamed in 1911 when it was moved from Fort Gibson and housed in the former Spaulding College building. In 1914, after former Governor Haskell donated a 25-acre site, a huge new building was erected to house the institution, and Helen Keller visited there the following year. By the post-war period it had record enrollments and was serving all of Oklahoma.

Another national influence reaching Muskogee was the so-called Red Scare of 1919-1920, an outgrowth of the Russian Revolu-

A World War I era military parade in downtown Muskogee. Courtesy of the family of Guy Fulenwider and Okie's Restaurant.

The Iowa Building which housed a variety of businesses, including the Muskogee National Bank, Schmitt Dry Goods, the Anicker Company, G. F. Bucher (real estate) and C. S. Bucher (lawyer), and the Iowa Land and Trust Company. Note the food vendor with his stand in front of the building. Courtesy Five Civilized Tribes Museum.

96

tion and fear of the spread of Bolshevism (as communism often was called). A radical labor union, the International Workers of the World (called the I.W.W.), had opposed American efforts during World War I and contributed to a feeling that some citizens were being infected with ideas foreign to the American political, educational, and social system. Ed Hirsh, president of the Muskogee Council, Boy Scouts of America, reflected this fear in October of 1919 when he commented, "The lessons and the life of the Boy Scouts form the most efficient arm of education in making the country free from the influence of the radical elements in these trying days of I.W.W. and Bolshevism."

Disturbing the economy of Muskogee County during the immediate post-war era was the agricultural depression which settled on the United States in 1919 and which would last until the outbreak of World War II. The price of cotton, beef, and other commodities fell disastrously. Wheat farming, which had boomed briefly in Muskogee County during the war when prices rose to new heights, virtually disappeared, and cotton again became king—and would remain so during most of the 1920s and 1930s. The percentage of farmland devoted to cotton production rose to 45 percent by 1924, then gradually slipped until by 1935 it was only 37.5 percent. The number of horses and mules gradually diminished as the tractor became an increasingly familiar sight.

Farmers entered an era of hard times that saw large-scale increases in the number of foreclosed mortgages, sheriff's sales, and tenant farming. Naturally this caused land prices to drop, as well as reduced the amount of money available for purchasing goods in the city. This, coupled with the increasing ease of driving into Muskogee, meant that the villages and towns in the County would begin to wither in numbers. Another by-product of the hard times was the closing of several banks in Muskogee.

All these changes were reflected in the census of 1920, which proved a strong shock. The County, which had grown so dramatically to 1910, when it had 52,743 residents, could find only 61,710 people within its borders in 1920. And Muskogee, which numbered 25,278 in 1910, had grown only to 30,277 a decade later. Tulsa increasingly would be the metropolis of eastern Oklahoma, its population booming from 18,182 in 1910 to 72,075 in 1920; as the self-proclaimed "Oil Capital of the United States," it would grow because it was not dependent on agriculture.

There would be some economic progress in Muskogee during the first half of the 1920s, but the pace of this growth was dramatically slower. Attempts continued to make the Arkansas safe for steam navigation. Hatbox Field was opened to handle airplanes, which could be seen in the sky above Muskogee with growing frequency. Promoting aviation locally was A. W. Hayes, who moved to Muskogee from his native Arkansas and established a chain of general and grocery stores.

Hatbox Field also received a boost when on September 18, 1924, three Army fliers making a trip around the world stopped at the Muskogee airport and were greeted by a crowd estimated at

Judge (Governor) Robert L. Williams. Courtesy Archives/Manuscript Division, Oklahoma Historical Society.

A humorous postcard entitled "A kiss from Webber's Falls Oklahoma" no doubt encouraged many young men to visit that community. Courtesy Sara Jo Wilson.

25,000; almost every activity in Muskogee shut down as people turned out at Hatbox to give a rousing welcome to the intrepid airmen. Three years later, after his historic flight across the Atlantic, Charles Lindbergh would say it was one of the best airports in the nation when he came to town (and proved the greatest attraction at the Fair that year).

Other evidences of maturity and steady growth were at every hand. The Kiwanis would organize locally, and Nick Paulos arrived in 1920 to open his first restaurant. The Melton (Muskogee) Hotel opened in 1922, and Hardin and Lee Nelson began what would grow into a major retailer of furniture that year. Muskogee Junior College opened its doors to the public, Bessie Huff joining the faculty in 1923 (soon its many graduates would refer to it as "Bessie Huff University"). The Griffin Grocery Company opened a new $150,000 facility in December of 1923 prior to J. T. Griffin moving

Employees of the Teel Laundry pose in front of that establishment with the delivery trucks in 1920. Courtesy C. W. "Dub" West.

the company headquarters from McAlester the following year; a leading wholesaler of groceries, the firm also manufactured many lines of products. H. B. Egan, later joined by his son James, established the H. B. Egan Manufacturing Company in 1923 in his garage, making a "cold patch" with which to repair flat tires. Twelve years later he would begin making hot patches and would advertise around the world. And the Bebb family arrived to open a floral shop and nursery; eventually five generations of this family would contribute to the economy of the city and County. Other noteworthy civic and economic boosters of this period were W. E. Rowsey and Paul Bruner.

Social change in Muskogee during this era was more dramatic than the economic slowdown. Nationally this was a time of marathon dances, flagpole sitting, bathtub gin, flapper dresses, "kissproof" lipstick, bobbed hair, and cigarette smoking. Dresses

Above: Alice M. Robertson as she appeared during her term in Congress. Courtesy Archives/Manuscript Division, Oklahoma Historical Society.

The Missouri Building housed the Missouri Hotel, the Muskogee Gas and Electric Company, and the Davis-Ogilvie Hardware Company. Courtesy Five Civilized Tribes Museum.

The New Phoenix Building. Note the electric sign on top which could be seen for miles. Courtesy Barbara Higbee Collection.

The Kress Store in Muskogee, located between Okmulgee and Broadway on the west side of Second Street. Courtesy Barbara Higbee Collection.

suddenly seemed too short and too tight, women were smoking in public, and dances and movies attracted the evenings—and even Sundays—of many people. Although Oklahoma had been dry since statehood, illegal moonshine whiskey was readily available. The *Phoenix* reported in August of 1920 that wagon loads of whiskey, drawn from the Cooksons by mules, were coming down from Belle Starr Canyon to the highway where they were met by trucks. Such activity matched a sudden rise in crime as outlaws fled to hideouts in the Cookson Hills where they were safe from law enforcement agents.

To conservative, Protestant Muskogeeans, these cultural changes seemed spawned by the devil to lure the young away from traditional values. Thus there were ready listeners when an organizer for the Ku Klux Klan arrived in Muskogee in February of 1921 to preach a return to the old-time verities and an end to crime. A local branch was soon founded, as also was a women's auxiliary, and during the next two years many well-intentioned and well-meaning citizens took the oath to this organization despite its condemnation by the Muskogee County Bar Association. In the summer of 1922 the strength of the Klan was such that 5000 members gathered at a site only five miles south of town, and the next day's newspaper carried a long story about the large number initiated that evening. Robed and masked Klansmen marched in city parades and made other public appearances, and there was a Klan meeting hall in town as if it were a normal civic club.

However, the brutal nature of the Klan gradually became increasingly evident, and the better element began to withdraw from it. On January 14, 1924, the state legislature passed a public anti-mask law, and the Klan quickly lost influence. By 1926 the organization had virtually ceased to exist. By this time Muskogeeans had other things to worry about—most notably the increasing economic hard times. The Great Depression might not settle on the United States until October of 1929, but it came sooner to eastern Oklahoma.

The Flynn-Ames Building. Courtesy Five Civilized Tribes Museum.

A view of Muskogee's business district, looking west from the Estes Building. Note the offices of Dr. G. L. Knebel, "Painless Dentist," in the foreground. Courtesy Five Civilized Tribes Museum.

Chapter Seven

DEPRESSION AND WAR

Within minutes after the Commercial National Bank opened its doors on February 10, 1926, a line began to form as rumors spread through town that the firm was about to fail. By 1:30 that afternoon the mood of the crowd began to turn ugly as they demanded their money. They knew that only a week before a bank at nearby Stigler had failed. The long-time president of the bank came outside to say that the rumor had been started by "a cowardly, contemptible, damnable, dastardly sneak" who was angry at not getting a loan. That evening and the next day the town's leaders rallied to support the Commercial, and it weathered the storm, after which it was reogranized by J. F. Darby and C. F. Lynde with Louis W. Duncan as president.

The Commercial soon would return to economic health, but its near collapse was a result of an agricultural depression settling on Muskogee County—and was a portent of what the next decade and more would be for both town and County. Farmers would see the price of cotton fall to five cents a pound by 1929, and by 1930 71.5 percent of those engaged in agriculture were tenant farmers. Each spring they went to country merchants or to one of the three surviving banks in Muskogee (the First, the Commercial, and Citizens) to borrow sufficient funds to get through until crops were harvested in the fall, at which time they prayed there would be enough on hand to pay off the bills. Such would not be the case in some years, for, as Elma Kilgore, a cotton buyer during that era, recalls, he once paid only $10 for a bale of cotton—two cents a pound.

The size of the average farm in Muskogee County had fallen from 100.5 acres in 1910 to 86.5 acres by 1930, while the value of the average farm, because of the agricultural depression which began at the end of World War I, had fallen from $6181 in 1920 to $2043 by 1935. During this era of record low prices for cotton, corn increasingly was grown; in 1934 cotton was raised on 37.5 percent of all land devoted to farming, while corn was on 30.7 percent, with alfalfa a distant third at 19.4 percent. The number of horses had diminished slightly to an average of 5.2 per farm, while the number of hogs, chickens, and milk cows had remained fairly constant.

County agents increasingly tried to teach scientific, diversified farming, while the FFA (Future Farmers of America), 4-H clubs sought to improve life for youngsters, most of whom were facing longer distances to attend schools that were consolidating. For most of these youngsters, the biggest event of the year would be the State Free Fair in Muskogee each autumn where they showed their animals and their other projects in competition for ribbons and prizes, where they ate hotdogs and cotton candy, and where they sampled the attractions of the midway. The rest of the year was a dreary repetition of hard work and little money, of loneliness and isolation, of watching neighbors lose their farms and move either into Muskogee or off to some far distant town to become a worker in some factory. The day of the family farm was passing, al-

Facing page: The Dough Boy statue in front of the Veterans Hospital at Muskogee. The statue was placed to commemorate members of the Five Civilized Tribes who died for their country during the first World War. At the base of the statue, left: Bess Davis Kiker; Mrs. Allece Locke Garrard of Mc-Alester who unveiled the statue and read a poem written by her father, Captain Ben D. Locke; Maude Davis Jones, who along with Mrs. Kiker, are aunts of Allece Garrard's and participated in the program. Courtesy Five Civilized Tribes Museum.

though hardy residents of Muskogee County would resist as long as possible.

Those farmers who survived did so by increasing the size of their fields and by converting from mule and horse power to the new tractors and other power machinery available. Moreover, the number of cattle in the County steadily grew as those involved in agriculture came to realize that Muskogee County indeed was on a prairie which nature had deemed best suited to the growing of grass. Herefords, Angus, and dairy cattle were brought in to crop the grass that once had fed buffalo, although truck crops, alfalfa, and cotton continued to be profitable on bottomland—those fields located near creeks and rivers where across the centuries the over-flow had deposited deep layers of silt.

Farm output increasingly was hauled to market not in the small towns of the County but to Muskogee itself where train and truck service was readily available. Braggs, Boynton, Haskell, Oktaha, Porum, Warner, and Webbers Falls became little more than cross-roads points where there were independent school districts, a post office, a few stores, perhaps a gin, and a population largely of older persons. Some of the young left for college and never came back to live, while others sought jobs in distant cities. They came home for Thanksgiving, Christmas, and reunions of their high school classes, the home town becoming little more than a misty, nostalgic memory of small-town America in their minds.

Life on the farm and in these small towns was gradually growing slightly better, however, for rural electrification would arrive in the 1930s, allowing almost every family to have modern lighting and a fan that stirred the hot air of summer. When homes were

The agricultural community of Haskell as it appeared in the late 1940s. Courtesy Marguerite Beshara.

wired for electricity, families acquired a radio in order to listen to music, soap operas, and news of the outside world provided by radio stations in Muskogee or even distant Tulsa. Rural telephone lines put County residents in touch with each other and the outside world, and better farm-to-market highways allowed easier access to town and city.

Fort Gibson fared slightly better than other small County towns during this period thanks to the efforts of its local citizens to restore the old Army post. In 1929 state legislator Q. B. Boydston, a prominent attorney in the region, introduced legislation to convey Sam Houston Park to the state and another bill to appropriate funds for reconstructing Fort Gibson to its former state. The legislation failed passage, but interested citizens, including Grant Foreman and Earl Boyd Pierce, got behind the project, and in 1935 the state appropriated $7500 and created the Old Fort Gibson Stockade Commission. Work began that summer, the total cost reaching $72,312; of this, the federal government contributed $55,791, the state $12,071, the town of Fort Gibson $3950, and the United Daughters of the Confederacy $500. Completed in 1938, the restored post then became a major tourist attraction. (In 1971 title to the fort passed to the State Parks Board, to be operated by the Oklahoma Tourism and Recreation Commission.)

Taft likewise would survive, thanks in large measure to the opening there of a state home for orphaned black children. Later this would become a state agency for children of all races, while Taft also would become the site of the Jess Dunn Correctional Center for delinquent children. These two agencies, one part of the State Department of Corrections, the other part of the Department

The Crystal Palace located near Irving School in Muskogee was one of the favorite hang-outs of the students from the 1920s into the 1950s. Former governor of Florida, Ruben Askew recalls the Crystal Palace with fondness as a place where he spent many hours during his youth. Courtesy Barbara Higbee Collection.

of Human Services, provided jobs for residents of Taft and the surrounding area.

Muskogee did not grow appreciably during the depression years prior to World War II. In the decade between 1920 and 1930 the increase in population was fewer than 2000 people to 32,026, while the census of 1940 was a severe disappointment as the counters could find only 32,314 residents, a gain of only 288 in a decade. Considering the economy in Oklahoma, Muskogee was faring well, however, for the state as a whole was losing population during these hard years. The discovery of vast oil fields, as at Seminole and Oklahoma City, created no great boom because the price of petroleum plummeted to historic lows. Factories closed as the market shrank for their output, and jobs became increasingly hard to find in cities such as Muskogee. Pure Oil Company would double the size of its refinery in Muskogee in 1926, but it suffered from the oil glut of the late 1920s and 1930s and gradually reduced its output. Muskogee businessmen participated in such federal New Deal programs as the National Recovery Administration (NRA), putting its blue eagle symbol in store windows; young men

The Federal Building at Muskogee in the late 1920s or early 1930s. Courtesy Archives/Manuscript Division, Oklahoma Historical Society.

found brief employment with the Civilian Conservation Corps (CCC), while adults took jobs with the Works Progress Administratin (WPA). Those who had relatives still on the farm fared best, for they could get food from the garden and smoke house.

Muskogee during this era was the cotton center of Oklahoma, almost all cotton in the state being wholesaled through the town. Elma Kilgore later would recall that during this era, when he represented one major buyer of cotton, his office filled one entire floor of the Railway Exchange Building, and he was employing some 25 secretaries to type the forms needed for federal purposes in the marketing of the cotton he bought.

During these hard years there were some construction projects that provided jobs and gave hope, such as Muskogee's new City Hall, which was built at a cost of $304,000 and dedicated on May 29, 1931. A new Administration Building opened at Bacone College in 1935, approximately the same time that the trolley tracks were removed in Muskogee as buses began to serve the transportation needs of the town. Another huge project was the spending of $900,000 to improve 185 miles of roads in Muskogee County in

A view of Hyde Park where Muskogeeans of an earlier age picnicked, frolicked, and courted. Courtesy Archives/Manuscript Division, Oklahoma Historical Society.

A view of Muskogee, showing how the railroad tracks split the town. Courtesy Archives/Manuscript Division, Oklahoma Historical Society.

1935. And in 1939 Cole Grain Company moved its offices to Muskogee, thereby providing some new jobs.

Yet during these hard years the quality of life in Muskogee continued to be high. The park gradually being developed on Agency Hill under the direction of G. W. Palmer became a showplace and in 1935 was awarded first prize by *Better Homes and Gardens* after a nationwide contest to find the most beautiful park in America.

The Hinton Theater, long the showplace of eastern Oklahoma, had been acquired by Fred Turner who operated it as the Orpheum until 1925 when he sold it to George Procter and Hugh Marsh of Muskogee and their partners in Dallas. The name was changed that year to the Ritz, and it operated as a vaudeville house until 1928 when it was equipped to show the new "talking" movies coming from Hollywood. During the 1930s Muskogeeans flocked to the movies, youngsters scheming all week to get the five cents necessary for admission to the Saturday matinee where Gene Autry or one of the other cowboy idols of that era would portray an Old West that never existed. Whenever some screen idol came to town, such as the visit by Tom Mix in 1929, crowds in the thousands turned out. The influences of the age were reflected in a newspaper poll in 1935 which revealed that Muskogee girls most

The Hinton Theater in Muskogee. On the stage of this theater appeared many names famous in American theatrical history. Courtesy Barbara Higbee Collection.

wanted to be like Shirley Temple and Muskogee lads most admired Charles Lindbergh.

The outbreak of war in Europe in 1939 brought some measure of returning prosperity to Muskogee County, as it did to the state and nation, as farm commodities and oil once again began to command high prices. By 1940 President Franklin D. Roosevelt and Congress began expanding the American armed forces, and Muskogee's lads rushed to the colors. Headlines in the *Phoenix* in June that year tell the story: "Uncle Sam's Rush Call for Pilots Summons Select Crew of Muskogeeans" and "Enlistment Boom Hits Muskogee."

Then in May of 1941 came an announcement that the Army would build a major training camp in the eastern part of the County just on the outskirts of Braggs and some 18 miles from Muskogee. Named Camp Gruber in honor of Brigadier General Edmund L. Gruber, author of "The Caisson Song" sung by artillerymen, the post was built by Manhattan Construction Company of Muskogee, headed by L. F. Rooney. It would open in 1942 and operate for four years, during which time some 80,000 young men would be trained there. Among these would be many artillerymen (on "Engineer Hill" there were stables for the mules that were used to pack small howitzers, and men were trained to fire these). The 42nd Infantry Division, known as the Rainbow Division because of its shoulder patch, prepared at Camp Gruber for the great battles the unit would fight in Europe. Built at a total cost of $30 million, the post at the height of its use contained some 2500 buildings, including five theaters, a giant swimming pool, a hospital, 12 chapels, 19 guardhouses, 221 recreation rooms, and 479 barracks. Muskogee also benefitted from the construction of Davis Army Air Field, an auxiliary landing strip where hundreds were stationed.

Camp Gruber and Davis Air Field proved a great economic stimulus to Muskogee as married servicemen sought housing in town and their children enrolled in local schools. Servicemen pumped tens of thousands of dollars into the local economy every month, creating new jobs, as did the building of the bases themselves. However, Muskogeeans gave back as much—if not more—than they received. Hundreds of local citizens volunteered to work at the local U.S.O. which sponsored dances, provided refresh-

Above: The band posing in front of the Muskogee Federal Building. Judging from the costumes and the symbols on the drum, perhaps this is a Shrine Band. Courtesy Barbara Higbee Collection.

Right: The Federal Building at Muskogee. Courtesy Five Civilized Tribes Museum.

ments, and offered wholesome entertainment to servicemen. Families invited soldiers to their homes for dinner, while the city's churches made special efforts to welcome servicemen each Sunday.

When the war began in December of 1941, Muskogeeans saw their sons—and not just a few of their daughters—joining the Armed Forces. Those who stayed at home became familiar with rationing stamps for the purchase of gasoline, meat, sugar, coffee, shoes, automobile parts, tires, and many other items. They participated in scrap iron drives, scouring city and County junk heaps and trash dumps for metal to be recycled into weapons of war. They grew "victory gardens" to conserve food, and they saved dimes and dollars to buy war stamps and bonds. More jobs were available and the economy was booming, but that was scant compensation for the casualty lists which grew to include if not a member of the family at least an old friend just down the block. Gold Star flags, indi-

The roller coaster at Hyde Park, recalled fondly by many Muskogeeans as the site of a great thrill in childhood. Courtesy Barbara Higbee Collection.

ROLLER COASTER AT HYDE PARK MUSKOGEE OKLA.

111

cating a family member killed in the war, were hung with pride and sorrow in many front windows across the County.

To replace the men gone off to war, women moved into the labor force in increasing numbers, and at war's end they would retain jobs held only by men previous to 1941. Few civilian goods were for sale in stores, and thus deposits grew at banks and savings and loan institutions. These would be available to fuel an economic boom when the war at last came to an end.

News of the Allied victory in Europe and in Japan caused wild celebrations in Muskogee during the summer of 1945, and there were parades and speeches as the County's young men and women returned from the fields of combat. Everyone hoped this conflict would usher in a long period of peace, and thus America's military forces quickly were reduced in size. By 1947 at deactivated

A view of Stem Beach in Honor Heights Park. Courtesy Five Civilized Tribes Museum.

Camp Gruber, grass was beginning to cover the scars of exploding artillery shells and even was growing in streets where thousands of combat boots had trod. Many soldiers who first saw the Three Forks area because they had been stationed at Camp Gruber would return to live in Muskogee because they had been impressed by the warm hospitality they had received from local citizens. The acres that had comprised Camp Gruber would be held by the Army as a potential training area for National Guard troops. Davis Army Air Field would be decommissioned and serve as a second airport for Muskogeeans, an increasing number of whom owned private aircraft.

Peace had returned, as always bringing with it new problems—and new challenges. Fortunately the city and County would produce leaders to move it forward toward a brighter future.

Modern Hatbox Field. Opened during World War I, this airport for many years was an Army Air Field. Today it serves a large number of private aviators and company pilots. Courtesy Jim Fowler.

Chapter Eight

TOWARD A BRIGHTER TOMORROW

At the end of World War II, Muskogee did not repeat the economic downturn that followed the end of the previous conflict. Camp Gruber and Davis Air Field would close, and by 1949 there again would be an agricultural depression, but the city would begin a process of slow, steady growth thanks to new leadership. Town fathers at last understood that Muskogee must be more than a wholesale and retail distributing point for the region and a market for agricultural commodities. If Muskogee was to regain the momentum it had enjoyed during the first decade of the 20th century, industry had to be attracted or developed locally, and a sustained effort began in this direction.

Shortly after World War II came to a close, Moon Inman, then executive director of the Muskogee Chamber of Commerce, heard that the Brockway Glass Company, of Brockway, Pennsylvania, might be interested in expanding its capacity, and he made contact with the firm. Eventually the president, vice president, and attorney for Brockway came to Muskogee to investigate the possibilities of locating a facility there. T. Elmer Harbour, president of the Chamber of Commerce, hosted a meeting at his home between these visitors and Inman, J. F. Darby, Hardin Nelson, and Louis

Facing page: West Broadway in Muskogee as it appeared in the 1950s. Courtesy Barbara Higbee Collection.

Left: The Five Civilized Tribes Museum as it appears today. Courtesy Jim Fowler.

115

Martha Watson Giffin and Jerome Tiger.
Courtesy Five Civilized Tribes Museum.

Duncan. After lengthy discussions, the Brockway officials said they would set up a plant in Muskogee if $250,000 in Brockway stock was sold locally. Eventually, thanks to the vision and foresight of investors in town, the stock was sold, some of it in lots as small as $100, and Brockway opened a plant in Muskogee that gave employment to hundreds.

A few years later came word that Corning Glass Works was opening plants in various parts of the country and was interested in a location in the southwestern part of the country. An invitation was delivered to officials of this firm to visit Muskogee, and afterward they indicated they would move to the city if they could get 25 acres on the north side of town at a reasonable cost. Twenty of those acres were owned by one man who agreed to sell; the remaining five acres was split up into several lots on which small homes had been built. Louis Duncan and Hardin Nelson, then president of the Muskogee Chamber of Commerce, spent several evenings coaxing these owners to sell. When they succeeded, Corning opened a plant providing employment and turning out a product sold nationwide.

The difficulty of acquiring land for industrial sites was solved permanently as a result of near economic disaster for Muskogee. In 1950 the Veterans Administration announced that it was being wooed by Oklahoma City to move its Muskogee hospital to the state capital. When pressed to keep the facility in Muskogee, the local administrator said the facility would remain only if additional office space was found for it. Town leaders, in searching for suitable space, learned that there was a vacant eight-story structure in town, the Railway Exchange Building. It was owned by a man in St. Louis who, when contacted, said he would sell the structure for $95,000.

Concerned individuals conceived the idea of raising the money privately, purchasing the building, and offering it free to the Veterans Administration if the hospital in Muskogee stayed put. After lengthy solicitations, the money was raised, and the Veterans Administration Hospital, with its healthy payroll, stayed in Muskogee. Several months later, after passage of a bond issue, the city repaid the donors, who thereupon contributed it to establish the Muskogee Industrial Foundation. With this money the Foundation sought additional industries, such as an electrical firm for which a structure was erected on the north side of town. When that firm

In 1948 at the centennial of the International Indian Exposition, the seals of the Five Civilized Tribes were painted on the streets of downtown Muskogee, along with the seal of the State of Oklahoma. Courtesy C. W. "Dub" West.

failed, its building was sold to James C. Leake to house his antique automobile collection, which became a major tourist attraction.

The board members of the Industrial Foundation soon discovered that one of the most difficult tasks they faced was securing land when a new industry wanted to locate in Muskogee. To insure long-range growth, the Foundation purchased 128 acres on the north side of town for $250 an acre, then broke this into smaller tracts as needed and sold it at reasonable cost to new businesses as needed. Then the Foundation persuaded the federal government to part with 500 acres at $500 an acre on the east side of town (north of Chandler Road) for a chemical plant. When this failed to open, the land was used to house other industries, such as Fort Howard Paper, which did move to Muskogee.

The Foundation also purchased the old Muskogee Electric Traction Company's car barn, located on 10 acres in the northeast part of town. Part of this later was sold to Bush Canning Company, which opened a plant operating on a year-round basis, and the remaining part of the site was sold to Corning Glass for use as a future warehouse. Other noteworthy additions to the local economy during this period included Callery Chemical.

In addition to bringing new industries to town, the Foundation

J. W. McLean is but one of the many Muskogeeans inducted into the Oklahoma Hall of Fame. A nationally prominent banker, he is chairman of the board of Liberty National Bank and Trust Company of Oklahoma City. Courtesy Liberty National Bank and Trust Company, Oklahoma City.

119

"The Stickball Player," a bronze statue by Jerome Tiger, is only one of many treasures housed in the Five Civilized Tribes Museum. Courtesy Five Civilized Tribes Museum.

also helped struggling local infant industries, such as Coburn Optical Company. O. W. Coburn had moved to Muskogee in 1950 to manage a local optical laboratory but the following year decided to quit and begin manufacturing one piece of optical equipment in his garage. Soon he expanded into an abandoned store on Second Street. In the next 24 years aided by low-interest loans from the Foundation and from a local bank, Coburn, his brother John, and the leadership team they assembled, astonished the optical world by surging into a position of leadership in the industry. Thereby it provided employment for hundreds of Muskogeeans, pumped millions of dollars into the local economy, and made possible O. W. Coburn's philanthropy to the city, state, and nation.

Also aiding in this industrial growth, in addition to the Muskogee Industrial Foundation, were excellent transportation facilities and a pool of qualified labor anxious to earn a day's wages and willing to give a day's work in return. Muskogee always had enjoyed excellent rail facilities, which had been supplemented by a growing network of fine state and national highways. By the 1960s, just as railroads everywhere were facing hard times and beginning

Frances Rosser Brown, Muskogee, under the direction of the Da-Co-Tah Indian Club, has been a leader in the development of The Five Civilized Tribes Museum. She is a member of the Oklahoma Hall of Fame. Portrait by Gloria Schumann.

to close operations, the McClellan-Kerr Waterway, a federal project, opened the Arkansas River to navigation to barges. This project long had been pushed by Harold Scoggins, who believed the task could be accomplished. Thanks to dredging, the creation of man-made lakes, and an intricate system of locks, river traffic again linked Muskogee and New Orleans. The Port of Muskogee was created—the first port city so designated in Oklahoma—and was a proving ground for other ports along the Waterway. From it would go industrial products, as well as coal and agricultural commodities. In addition, the Muskogee Turnpike, a toll road from Tulsa to Muskogee to a junction with Interstate 40 some 20 miles to the south, was opened in 1970 and made truck transportation easier to the region.

The Indian Capital Area Vocational-Technical school opened in Muskogee, after local citizens voted a bond issue and a millage tax, to train workers for the new industries coming to town. A large percentage of those enrolling for training were not recent high school graduates, but rather adults seeking skills that would qualify them for good employment. An astonishing percentage of the

122

workers in Muskogee's industrial plants were former agricultural laborers, for the pre-war trend of fewer but larger farms in the County accelerated in the 1950s and 1960s. In fact, there was increasing recognition that Muskogee County with few exceptions was best suited to ranching.

Around the Three Forks area on bottom land, farmers would continue to raise truck produce, and on selected acres hay and other crops could be grown, but for the most part Muskogee County was returning to grass. King Cotton was not dead, but he was badly wounded. Fescue and Bermuda were planted to replace the blue stem and gramma grasses that had been plowed under, and Hereford, Angus, and Charolais cattle were put to grazing where cotton once had been raised. Commercial and purebred ranching became a prominent part of agriculture in Muskogee County, supplying beef to a nation that had an increasing appetite for it.

Whether residents of Muskogee County lived in town or remained on the land, the quality of life improved dramatically during the post-war period. Rural electrification, the extension of telephone lines, and a fine system of county paved roads made transportation and communication easy. Anyone in the County could be in downtown Muskogee in only a matter of minutes, so all could shop in the same stores, work at similar employment, and enjoy the same recreational facilities.

Facing page: Willard Stone, a nationally prominent Cherokee wood sculptor. A member of the Oklahoma Hall of Fame, Stone is a native of Oktaha. Courtesy Oklahoma Heritage Association.

Left: Barge Traffic on the Arkansas River. Perhaps not as romantic as the days of early steamboating on the Arkansas, the present system, maintained by the U. S. Army's Corps of Engineers provides a major outlet for coal mined in Muskogee County. Courtesy Jim Fowler.

Above: J. Howard Edmondson of Muskogee, who became Oklahoma's youngest governor in 1960. Courtesy Oklahoma Heritage Association.

Below: The W. D. Mayo Lock and Dam #14 on the Arkansas River Navigation System near Spiro. A load of steel pipe destined for the port of Muskogee is being moved up the system by the barge. This was the first commercial shipping and barge passing through the first lock on the system near Spiro at 2:45 P.M., January 2nd, 1971. Courtesy Barbara Higbee Collection.

There were changes in the pattern of recreation during this era as television replaced movies as the prime source of entertainment. In 1954 Muskogee received a license for television station KTUL, but within a few years this moved to Tulsa; however, it still is owned locally and is readily received in all homes in the County, as are the other Tulsa stations, while two radio stations in Muskogee keep citizens informed and entertained at all times.

The system of man-made lakes, created to keep the water at a constant level in the McClellan-Kerr Waterway, have made fishing and boating readily available to everyone in the County. The Grand River was dammed a few miles above Fort Gibson, creating Fort Gibson Reservoir, while Lakes Eufaula, Greenleaf, and Tenkiller were just half an hour away by automobile.

Another improvement in the quality of life in the County has been air conditioning, which became widely available to even low-income families in the years following World War II. It no longer was necessary for affluent families to summer in Minnesota or Colorado, for most homes and automobiles were climate controlled, as were shops and stores—and the three shopping centers opened in Muskogee: Lakeland Shopping Center on Eastside Boulevard, which opened in 1962; Honor Heights Plaza on the west side of town, developed by O. W. Coburn; and B. S. Curtsinger's Curt's Mall, which is on the north side of the city. Downtown merchants fought the trend to suburban shopping by redoing both interiors and exteriors of their establishments, creating a new beauty in the downtown area and providing yet more comfort and convenience for shoppers.

Improving the quality of life in Muskogee, as well as bringing hundreds of thousands of dollars into the economy of Muskogee has been Honor Heights Park. Opened in 1921 to honor those who served in World War I, the Park came under the direction of Arthur C. "Art" Johnson in 1948. He planted it with azaleas in a rainbow of colors, some 35,000 of them from 625 different varieties. In addition, the area was planted with some 17,000 rosebushes of more than 420 varieties, adding to the color and beauty. In 1967 the Park Department began promoting a spring Azalea Festival to attract visitors, and that year some 50,000 people came to see the riot of beauty blooming on Agency Hill. By 1982 the spring Azalea Festival was attracting 600,000 visitors from 40 states and many foreign countries. Townspeople, realizing the value of this festival, organized the Hospitality Committee to insure that visitors have a pleasant stay in town. Since Art Johnson's retirement, Henry Bresser, as director of the Park, has continued the same high standards of beauty and excellence.

Other tourist attractions in the County include the Five Civilized Tribes Museum, housed in the old Union Agency and dedicated to preserving the artifacts and aesthetic contributions of Native Americans from the Creek, Cherokee, Choctaw, Chickasaw, and Seminole Nations; the *U.S.S. Batfish*, a submarine involved in many battles in World War II, which is permanently anchored north of the city near the Port of Muskogee; the Thomas-Foreman Home, built by Judge John Thomas in 1898 and the residence for many years of his daughter Carolyn and her lawyer-historian husband Grant Foreman; James Leake's Horseless Carriage Museum;

A view of the restored Fort Gibson. Courtesy Archives/Manuscript Division, Oklahoma Historical Society.

and the restored Fort Gibson Stockade just a few minutes' drive to the east. Bacone College, which celebrated its 100th anniversary in 1980, likewise draws visitors to see its excellent collection of Indian paintings—and continues to serve the area with educational opportunities, as does Connors State College at Warner.

The census of 1980 showed that Muskogee County had grown to 66,139 residents, while the city could count 40,011 inside its 22.5 square miles. Through dedication and hard work, as well as a willingness to tax themselves for the betterment of the community, Muskogeeans have revitalized their city. In 1967 a Fine Arts Auditorium was completed, and the following year a new Civic Center complex was opened. And in 1972 came completion of a new public library. These have transformed the downtown area and provided convention facilities where 4000 can be seated.

In the early 1970s, while the United States was undergoing social unrest and change, Country-Western singer Merle Haggard had a hit record of epic proportions entitled "Okie From Muskogee" in which he said that the town clung to its traditional values, that drugs were not part of the local culture, and that everyone, even the children, still respected authority. Unfortunately Haggard was not totally correct, for Muskogee has shared in the changes—both good and bad—that have come in national values and attitudes.

Yet Muskogeeans have not totally turned their backs on the historic regional beliefs of work, thrift, and virtue. They still see the beauty and bounty of Nature in the area around the Three Forks. They have loved their country and have served it by sending their sons and daughters to fight in two additional wars, the Korean Conflict, and the heartbreaking struggle in far-off Viet Nam. They still stand to salute the flag, and they sing the National Anthem when their high school sons and daughters engage in athletic contests. They still work hard all week, cherish their friends, pay their bills and their taxes as they struggle to raise families, and worship the God of their fathers on Sunday morning. So long as these traits from a unique heritage endure, the sacrifices of pioneers—red, black, and white—will not have been in vain.

Muskogeeans in their long history have met and overcome hardship and heartbreak as their County provided a home to diverse people. Its residents have hoped and dreamed, laughed and cried, prayed and endured as they built a better future for themselves and for those who came after them. Present and future residents of the historic County in the Three Forks area can afford to do no less.

Facing page, top: The U. S. Batfish, a World War II combat submarine permanently anchored just north of Muskogee on the Arkansas River. Bottom: Downtown Muskogee today. Both courtesy Jim Fowler.

LAND OF BEAUTY,
LAND OF DREAMS

Muskogee—city and County—home to diverse
people in its long and colorful history has a
unique heritage. Attempting to preserve this history is
the Five Civilized Tribes Museum, housed in the old
Union Agency building on Honor Heights. Through
the dediction of Peggy Denton, her staff, and the
volunteers who contribute both time and money, the
Five Civilized Tribes Museum has built one of the
finest collections of Native American art in existence,
annually holding a respected refereed show, and it has
gathered artifacts relating to the history and culture of
the Five Civilized Tribes. All of the paintings in the
section which follows are the property of the Five
Civilized Tribes Museum, as are all of the artifacts
shown. Muskogee indeed has become the cultural—as
well as economic—capital of eastern Oklahoma. The
color photography was done by Jim Fowler of
Muskogee.

Museum Seal designed by
Solomon McCombs
Chosen from 55 entries
in Museum Seal Contest, 1956.
Donor: Solomon McCombs

Sticks — Creek and Cherokee — used in stickball game by all five Tribes. From collection of Five Civilized Tribes. Inset: Deer hide ball — used to play stickball. From the collections of the Five Civilized Tribes Museum.

"Meadow Lark"
Troy Anderson - Cherokee

131

Lazy Z Branding Iron - Brand of Bill Brown, Cherokee Nation Donor: John C. Brown, (son) Ft. Gibson, Oklahoma

Bar Muleshoe branding iron from Judge N. B. Moore ranch. Donor: Judge Thomas E. Moore and Kenneth D. Moore

I J Branding iron from Hammons ranch near Webbers Falls, established 1887. Donor: Edith Hammons Morgan

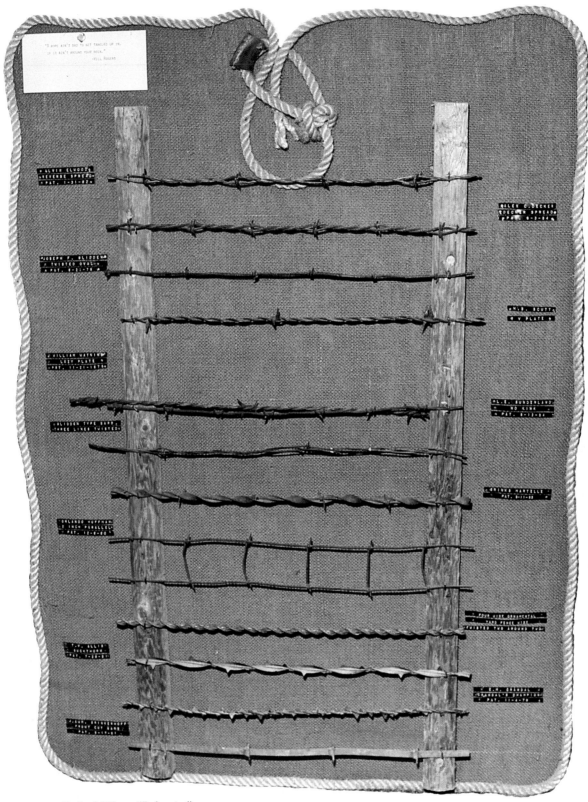

Barbed Wire - "Bob-wire"
used in Indian Territory.
Donor: Arthur C. Johnson

"Night Stomp Dance"
Fred Beaver-Creek

Union Agency, Indian Territory Safe.
Donor: Bureau of Indian Affairs

"Unending Journey"
Valjean M. Hessing - Choctaw

Bucket Grill -
purchased at Patterson Mercantile
Donor' Malcolm E. Rosser

Wooden Washboard, hand made
Donor: Oma Irving and daughter
Juliana Hiner in memory of Watie Irving

Cherokee Kanuchi stump,
used for pounding hickory nuts and corn.
Donor: Wynona G. Daywood.

138   *Saddle - Wm. N. Patterson, territory
merchant. Donor: Children of Wm. N.
Patterson; Catherine Patterson Stuart,
Mary Pattersoon Fite, William N.
Patterson, Jr.*

*"He Marked The Warriors" - Brass
Saint Clair Homer - Choctaw & Chickasaw*

HE MARKED THE WARRIORS

Creek Sofkee spoon
Donor: Dr. O. C. Hinkle

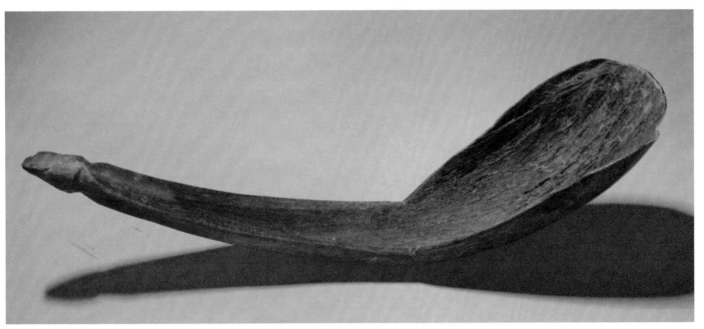

Horn Spoon
Donor: Miss Alice Joseph

"Whispers On The Trail"
Bert Seabourn - Cherokee

141

The Muskogee Azalea Festival
Photo courtesy Jim Argo.

"And On The Seventh Day"
Joan Hill - Creek & Cherokee

143

*Scale - used by soldiers
when purchasing grain for Fort Gibson*

"Uprooted" Cedar Stump
Willard Stone

"The Offspring" - Walnut Wood
Jason Stone - Cherokee

145

"Owl Legend"
Enoch Kelly Haney - Seminole

146

*Two Creek Indian dolls,
handmade in 1893.
Donor: Helen Briggs Plato*

"Giants Of The Woodlands"
Solomon McCombs - Creek

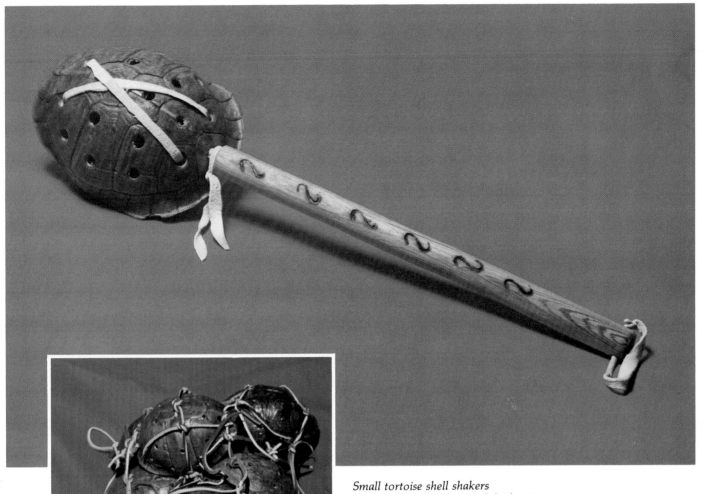

Small tortoise shell shakers
carried in hand by men while dancing.
From collection of Five Civilized Tribes Museum. Creek

Shell shackles - lace on women's legs
for dancing.
From collection of Five Civilized Tribes
Museum. Creek

"Good Omen"
Johnny Tiger Jr. - Creek & Seminole

Boundary line marker
between Creek and Cherokee Nations.
Donor: Muskogee County Commissioners

Cornerstone — Fountain Church, I. T.
Established in 1832, original site now
inundated by Arkansas River navigation channel.

Glass Compote which belonged to Miss Alice Robertson, Missionary to Creek Indians, first Congresswoman from Oklahoma and Muskogee Postmistress. From collection of Five Civilized Tribes Museum

"Wild Deer"
Acee Blue Eagle - Creek

The historic Three Forks Area today.

Bell from Sally Brown School
Donor: Jon Tom Staton

"High Country"
Bob Bell

"Choctaw Fire Curer" Chief
Terry Saul-Choctaw & Chickasaw

Bull tongue for plow, from old Asbury Mission site near Eufaula.
Donor: Don Bankston

Handmade Carpenter's tools, planes used for coffin making.
Donor: Juliana Hiner

Buffalo Head
Donor: Bureau of Indian Affairs

Gun used by Belle Starr,
notorious woman outlaw.
Donor: C. L. Oglesbee, M.D.

Rifle, 1895 model Winchester,
owned by James F. (Uncle Bud) Ledbetter
Donor: John Ledbetter

"Broken Dreams"
Troy Anderson - Cherokee

"War to Peace, Death to Life"
Jerome Tiger — Creek-Seminole

BUILDERS OF GREATER MUSKOGEE

Muskogee was conceived in the sorrow of the Native American and born when steel rails bridged the muddy Arkansas River. As it matured, it was flavored by a mixture of hide and horn, of farmers' unremitting toil, and of pioneer merchants' vision. Muskogee—city and county—has been blessed with extraordinary talent in diverse fields, people who hoped and dreamed, who built and created, and who have been willing to contribute to projects the pessimists said could "never be done."

There is a common thread in each of the success stories that follows: the opportunity which Muskogee offered—and still offers—to those willing to dream large dreams and then to take risks in the free marketplace to transform dream into reality. Wives worked with husbands, children with parents, and the result has been of great benefit to all residents of the county, state, and nation.

AMERICAN SAVINGS
AND INVESTMENT CORPORATION

W. H. Gilder, Sr.

W. H. Gilder, Jr.

A. Earnest Gilder.

The American Savings and Investment Corporation originally was established as the Muskogee Industrial Finance Corporation on April 1, 1925, at the corner of Fourth and Wall streets. On August 1, 1978, the corporate name was changed to American Savings and Investment Corporation.

The original incorporators were Dr. F. E. L. Thomas, Dr. E. E. Overmyer, and J. L. Hanner with $100,000 of common stock, $10,000 of the original stock issued. The corporation has grown until current assets are in excess of $6.5 million. Some of the corporation's current stockholders are the fourth generation of families who were original stockholders.

A branch office was opened in McAlester in October of 1929 on the Monday following the great stock market crash. The first office manager was Joe Wolfenberger, son of E. R. Wolfenberger, who later would serve as president of the corporation.

In 1933 a building was purchased at 412 Court Street, and the following year, after a complete remodeling of the building, the corporation moved into its new—and present—location. That same year of 1934 a vacant lot adjoining the main office was purchased, and in 1950 a drive-through facility was installed on this lot.

Another branch office was opened in Ada in 1935, a third in Pryor in 1955, and a fourth in Sand Springs (as the Sand Springs Finance Company) in 1964.

The principle lines of business of American Savings and Investment Corporation are consumer lending, commercial and real estate loans, and a complete savings program which includes money market certificates, certificates of deposit, and passbook savings.

Presidents of American Savings and Investment Corporation have been: Harry E. West, 1925-1937; E. R. Wolfenberger, 1938-1941; Carl K. Bates, 1942-1972; and W. H. Gilder, Jr., 1973-present.

Current directors are: W. H. Gilder, Jr., A. Earnest Gilder, Maurine L. Gilder, Mary L. Huckin, Jim A. Egan, Dorothea Ruby, and Donna Beardsley.

Corporation officers are: W. H. Gilder, Jr., President; A. Earnest Gilder, Vice President; Donna Beardsley, Secretary; and Jim A. Egan, Treasurer.

Beginning with two employees in 1925, American Savings and Investment Corporation now has 12 employees in its main office in Muskogee and branch offices across Oklahoma.

Beginning small, the American Savings and Investment Corporation has grown and changed in an effort to better serve the needs of the growing and changing community of which it is a part.

ARKHOLA SAND AND GRAVEL COMPANY

Founded in 1911 as a two-shovel, two-wagon, two-man operation, the Arkhola Sand and Gravel Company by 1971 had grown to become one of the largest suppliers of concrete building materials in a two-state area.

When the Dills, Walter Scott, his wife Syrina Brothers Dills, and Charles Edward moved to Indian Territory from Greencastle Indiana, they first settled as farmers in Choska Bottoms near Yahola. In 1911 the brothers began hauling sand they shoveled from the Arkansas River bed to Robert Clements and Bill White in Muskogee. Within a few years the Dills formed a partnership with Clements, White, and Dr. "Pete" Nesbit, all of Muskogee, and incorporated the Yahola Sand and Gravel Company.

During the late teens, the company was moved to the Arkansas River near Goose Neck Bend, and a romance with the Arkansas began which eventually would touch almost everyone in eastern Oklahoma and Arkansas. It touches almost everyone because it is unlikely anyone could spend a day anywhere in the area without walking on, driving on, being sheltered by, or entering a home, commercial building, community building, hospital, office, apartment, or recreational area or even drink from a container that is not made, at least in part, from materials supplied by Arkhola.

About the same time the company moved to the Arkansas River, the partners bought the *City of Muskogee*, a paddle-wheel boat that would become Muskogee's first dredge boat. It also was during this time that they began delivering sand and gravel to their customers by electric train—the Muskogee Electric Traction Company—which ran from Goose Neck Bend to the York Street Station.

The company prospered in the late Teens and survived shortages created by World War I. Many of these shortages were overcome by the ingenuity and hard work of the Dills brothers. For example, at the end of the war, when there was a shortage of boxcars, the Dills simply built their own.

The beginning of the depression in the late Twenties had its effect on the Yahola Sand and Gravel Company. At times like that, Walter Dills supplemented his family's income by crop farming on the side in the Fort Gibson bottomlands.

In 1926 Walter's oldest son, William "Bill" Walter Dills joined the company. Bill was born in 1907, grew up in and around the Three Forks area, and graduated from high school in 1923 at age 16. The

The steamboat "Muskogee" was bought by Arkhola as a dredge boat.

other Dills children are: Robert S. "Bob," who would become the company president; Louise Dills Kroh, deceased; and another daughter who died in infancy.

The same year he joined the company, Bill was sent to Fort Smith to open a branch plant—the Arkhola Sand and Gravel Company. In 1936 Bob joined Bill in Fort Smith. The following year ready-mixed concrete was added to the growing list of materials supplied by the ever-expanding company.

Before enlisting in the United States Army in 1938, Bill traveled to Mexico and studied the customs and language of the Mexican people. By the time he returned to the United States, he spoke fluent Spanish. Bill continued his travels and made several private investments. During his tenure in the armed forces, most of which was served in the South Pacific, Bill rose to the rank of colonel in the 367th Engineering Regiment. Upon the death of his father, he returned to Muskogee and the now-incorporated Arkhola Sand and Gravel Company, headquartered in Fort Smith.

By the late 1950s Arkhola had entered other construction fields, such as rock crushing and asphaltic concrete. Most of the rock used to build the locks and dams that opened the Arkansas River to navigation, as well as the vast new network of Interstate Highways in the area, was taken from the limestone mine north of Fort Gibson which Bill had purchased in the early 1950s.

The 1960s would see many changes for Bill and for Arkhola Sand and Gravel. In 1960 Bill, an avid golfer, met Dena Logan Dobson, a widow with an eight-year-old son, Joey. Dena was at the Muskogee Country Club (of which Bill was president at the time of his death) to participate in the Women's Oklahoma State Golfing Championship when she and Bill met on the golf course. Bill and Dena were married in 1961, and a few years later Bill adopted Joey.

Joey Dobson Dills later would become the youngest person ever to win the State Junior High School Golf Championship. He was 14 at the time and would go on to become one of the top amateur golfers in the nation.

Another change taking place in the 1960s was the expansion of Arkhola, with plants being located in Little Rock, Van Buren, Springdale, Fayetteville, Rogers, Pine Bluff, and Eldorado in Arkansas, in addition to plants already in Fort Smith, Muskogee, and Fort Gibson.

In the mid-1960s Bill undertook and accomplished one of the most important projects of his life. Because the water in the Arkansas River contained large amounts of iron, the sand taken from the river was not suitable for use in the manufacturing of glass. Bill realized opportunity and progress were being lost because of this. It became his goal to perfect a formula and a device to take the iron from the sand and thus make it possible to produce silica used in manufacturing glass. After years of patient struggle, Bill, with the assistance of a chemist in Reno, Nevada, succeeded. The formula and device were perfected and are now protected by patent.

Shortly after this accomplishment, the Arkhola Sand and Gravel Company was sold to Ashland Oil Company, but the Dills stayed with the company on a consulting basis for three years after the sale—until Bill's death in April of 1971. Bill served as Chairman of the Board and Chief Operations Officer, and Bob was President.

It is difficult to believe that a two-mule, two-man operation that began in 1911 would grow to become a giant in the construction industry which, by the time of its sale, would operate plants in a dozen cities, stockpile and ship materials throughout the United States and 14 foreign countries, employ more than 300 people, have investments along the Arkansas River representing almost $2 million, and annual sales in excess of $20 million—indeed a fairy tale romance between a man and a river.

Joey Dobson Dills and William Walter Dills.

ANDERSON WHOLESALE

Anderson Wholesale began when John F. and Sue Anderson moved to Muskogee from Prague on March 15, 1949, after having purchased Ellis Distributing Company, a small operation selling sundries and notions to grocery stores. They employed three salesmen (including John), one driver, one warehouseman, and Sue, who managed the office and swept the floors.

The Anderson's oldest son, James Thomas "J. T.," joined the firm after graduating from Oklahoma State University in 1950. Three years later he married the former Barbara Lightle of Muskogee, and they have two sons, James Mark and Michael Kent.

John Francis, Jr., after graduating from local schools and Central Christian College in Bartlesville (later Oklahoma Christian College in Oklahoma City), also joined the family operation. In 1952 he married the former Anne McPhersosn of Oklahoma City, and they have three children: Susan Gaylyn, John Brent, and Janet Anne.

By the late 1950s the business that had started with an inventory of $8500 and occupied a 50 by 100 foot building at 114 Callahan had grown to such an extent that holes literally were knocked through walls to allow the young company access to other buildings. In 1950, when the firm moved into its new structure, it was occupying six adjoining buildings on Callahan Street and several garages behind these structures.

L. to R.: Mrs. John F. Anderson, James T. Anderson, John F. Anderson, Jr. Seated, John F. Anderson.

The new facility at 2211 West Shawnee By-Pass doubled Anderson's work area to a total of 24,000 square feet. Later additions, the last in 1981, gives the business 65,000 square feet of warehouse and office space, and there is property available for further expansion.

The business was incorporated in 1960 with all stock owned by John, Sue, and their two sons. Family members are officers and directors of the corporation. When John and Sue retired in 1975, J. T. assumed the responsibilities of president; John, Jr., became vice president; J. W. Thomas, one of the first employees, became secretary-treasurer and general manager; and William E. Smith, another initial employee, served as a member of the Anderson buying staff.

The firm employs 145 people at the Muskogee facility and has drop-off warehouses in Wichita, Kansas, Des Moines, Iowa, Joplin, Missouri, Oklahoma City, and Tulsa. Fifty-two salesmen, eight sales-supervisors, and five full-time buyers determine the products each store should stock, sticker price and place the items on shelves, and remove, replace, and rotate nonfood products for sale by the more than 1500 Anderson customers in Oklahoma, Arkansas, Kansas, Missouri, and Iowa.

This "service-merchandising" concept came to the grocery industry about the same time Anderson Wholesale began, making the Muskogee firm one of the pioneers in this type of marketing. To serve this multi-state industry more effectively, to attain more efficient bookkeeping and accounting, and to maintain a perpetual inventory of the approximately 10,000 items stocked in the warehouse, Anderson now is served by an IBM Systems 38.

Since the early 1960s, J. T. has had a role in the national trade organization for service merchandisers. He has held every office in Service Merchandisers of America and was named Chairman of the Board in 1976. He has remained active in the National Association of Service Merchandisers since its formation in 1979.

Anderson's future management team includes Jerry D. Frazier and John Paul Gilliam, in addition to third-generation family members Brent Anderson, Mark Anderson, and Mike Anderson.

BACONE COLLEGE

Oklahoma's oldest center of higher education—and the oldest college for Indian education in the United States—Bacone College began on February 9, 1880, at Cherokee Baptist Mission in Tahlequah, I.T. Known initially as the Indian University, its only faculty member was its founder, Almon C. Bacone, and its student enrollment was three.

From the school's beginning, Bacone wanted a more central location for The Indian University, and Muskogee, with its Union Agency for the Five Civilized Tribes, offered the most favorable site for the school in order for it to be identified with all tribes.

On October 29, 1881, the Creek (Muscogee) Tribal Council donated 160 acres of land as a permanent site for the university. The first building erected at the new location, Rockefeller Hall—named in honor of John D. Rockefeller, whose $10,000 donation made the building possible—was completed in the spring of 1885. In June that year the entire student body and faculty drove in wagons from Tahlequah to the new school in what came to be known as the "Great Removal."

Bacone continued growing during the last decade of the 19th century despite the death in 1896 of its president and founder, Almon C. Bacone. However, readjustments came with statehood and the introduction of public education in the new state, and Bacone's enrollment dropped to 110 students in 1909 from 158 the previous year. In 1909 the junior and senior years at the university were dropped from the curriculum, and in 1910 the name was changed to Bacone College.

From 1911 to 1916 there were no students taking courses beyond what is now considered the

Bacone Memorial Chapel.

high school level. Along with the rest of the country, the college struggled through the depression years before World War I, but experienced tremendous growth between the wars. By 1922 the student population had risen to 234 drawn from 24 tribes in five states. During this boom period, all new construction was in English style of red bricks and limestone. The buildings were erected in a line running north and south across the campus to intersect the east-west line already formed by Rockefeller and Sacajawea Halls. Thus the buildings formed the shape of a Christian cross.

In 1927 college-level courses were reinstituted, and in 1934 the Wheeler-Howard Act brought another dramatic change for Bacone. This act, changing the federal attitude toward Indians, was felt by the students and was reflected in activities and curricula during the decade. Native music, tribal customs and traditions, and costumes once again were introduced. Also during this period of national depression, Bacone made one of its

most important contributions to American culture by creating an art department which focused on and fostered what has come to be called the "Bacone School of Traditional Indian Art."

More than any other previous conflict or change, World War II caused enrollment to drop at Bacone. By the end of 1943 it had more than 160 students in the armed forces, all serving brilliantly, some giving their lives.

In 1957, in an effort to achieve accreditation, the preparatory school was eliminated. The space age meant a greater emphasis on math and science for college students and a corresponding lessening in emphasis on the liberal arts and classical studies, which had been Bacone's strongest areas. Nevertheless, Bacone continued to adjust, and was accredited by the North Central Association in 1965. During this time span, the college also emphasized its role of educating all who desired a higher education.

With accreditation and the closing of Muskogee Junior College in the early 1960s, Bacone became a comprehensive junior college, and with the introduction of new degree programs, such as nursing, it more nearly filled Muskogee's educational needs.

Today the campus is located on a 200-acre hilltop with 34 buildings. The student body ranges between 400 and 600 and is truly multicultural. Fifty-five tribes from 35 states frequently are represented at Bacone.

Under the leadership of Dr. Paul V. Moore, who became acting president in August of 1981, Bacone, beginning its second century in higher education, looks back on a distinguished past and excitedly anticipates a challenging future.

BRADLEY FUNERAL HOME, INC.

Muskogee's oldest funeral service under the same family ownership and management, Bradley Funeral Service, Inc., originated in 1905 as Eicholtz Funeral Home located in the 500 block of West Okmulgee.

That same year James S. and Mable Bradley moved from Crane, Missouri, to Muskogee, I.T. The family grew and prospered in their new home. Eight children were born to them, and within a few years the dairy farm they began in 1905 would become the largest in Muskogee County.

One of the Bradleys' sons, Dick, born on November 2, 1916, started to work on the dairy farm at age 15 when his father died on April 24, 1931. In 1939 Dick married a local girl, Madelene Treadway.

Dick and Madelene remained on the farm until April 1, 1941, when Dick went to work for the Eicholtz Funeral Home, which in 1939 had relocated on Callahan Street. In 1944 the name was changed to Hunter-Eicholtz and remained so until April 1, 1949, when Dick bought the business, incorporated it, and changed the name to Bradley Funeral Service, Inc. The total work force that year, including Dick, was three.

In 1957 Bradley Funeral Service moved to its third—and present—location at 1020 West Okmulgee.

Dick and Madelene had two children: Lynda Bradley Hudson, who died on January 2, 1969; and a son, Richard.

Richard grew up and attended school in Muskogee, then graduated from the University of Oklahoma in 1960 with a bachelor's degree in Fine Arts. After receiving his degree, Richard joined the faculty of East Central High School and taught speech, history, and English for six years.

In the fall of 1969, while doing

Dick Bradley.

Richard Bradley.

postgraduate work at the University of Tulsa, Richard worked for the Lowe Runkle Advertising Company and did the week-end weather for KTUL-TV.

On June 1, 1971, Richard married Leigh Maltby of Bartlesville. The Maltby family is prominent in Bartlesville, having owned and operated Maltby Hardware in that city for three generations (1900-1970).

In 1972 Richard and Leigh moved to Muskogee, and Richard joined his father in the family business. Richard and Leigh have four children: Carter, eight; Elizabeth-Leigh, seven; Jordan, four; and Ryan, two.

After joining the corporation in 1972, Richard attended and completed studies at the National Funeral Directors Management School in Evanston, Illinois. Today he is president and general manager of the corporation.

Just as Muskogee has changed in the past and will continue to change in the future, so has Bradley Funeral Service changed and will continue to change to give its community better service. Dick is Chairman of the Board and still remains active in the day-to-day operations, although Richard has assumed most of the responsibility for operation and management of the business. The work force has risen to eight. Facilities and equipment continually are updated and changed. But one thing never changing at Bradley Funeral Service is the dedicated service it has always given—and will give in the future—to the people of Muskogee in their time of greatest sorrow.

BRESSER NURSERY

Above: Bresser's first delivery truck. Left: L. to R.: Emil Bresser, Herman Bresser, Mother Bresser, Helen Bresser, Henry Bresser, Anthony Bresser, and Edith Bresser in 1909 just prior to moving to Muskogee from Toledo, Ohio.

Among the many points of interest Muskogee has to offer its residents and visitors, none is more breathtakingly beautiful than Azalea Park in Honor Heights Park. Muskogeeans and tourists from around the world flock to Muskogee annually to walk and drive through this exquisite paradise-of-a-thousand colors in early spring during the Muskogee Azalea Festival.

Although the Bressers had nothing directly to do with originating Azalea Park, they indirectly were instrumental in making it possible because it was Bresser Nursery which in 1940 first brought azaleas to Muskogee.

Bresser Nursery began in March of 1910 when Henry and Cecilia Bresser loaded their family, furniture, and tools onto a train in Toledo, Ohio, and departed for Muskogee. Henry, who had been sexton of Calvary Cemetery in Toledo, had visited Muskogee the year before and had decided the climate and location would be ideal for raising a family and plants.

The Bressers stayed at the Katy Hotel while they personally built their nine-room, one-story home

on the 10-acre plot of land Henry had purchased. At the same time the house was being constructed, Henry ordered three green houses and planted his first crop—lettuce. Other vegetables, such as tomatoes, cucumbers, broccoli, and turnips, also were soon being grown.

Within a few years the wholesale produce business Henry had started, delivering directly by wagon to grocers in Muskogee, expanded to include outlets in Okmulgee, Henryetta, and Wagoner. By 1920, however, because of increasing competition from larger truck farms and a drop in prices, Henry changed from growing vegetables to the retailing and wholesaling of flowers. Carnations were grown at first, but soon Bresser Nursery was producing hundreds of types of roses, mixed flowers, and bedding plants.

Also in the 1920s Bresser Nursery opened a retail office at 115 North 3rd Street. Henry's and Cecilia's daughters Edith and Helen operated the retail shop while their sons Tony, Emil, and Herman grew the plants. At the same time the retail outlet opened, Bressers also became a landscape and wholesale nursery. Evergreens were the

first nursery plants stocked by Bresser Nursery.

In 1940 the first azaleas were brought to Muskogee by Tony Bresser and his son Henry. Soon azaleas became the nursery's biggest seller. The market for these expanded to include Tulsa, McAlester, Oklahoma City, and Bartlesville. At one time 250,000 azaleas in 250 varieties were being grown by Bresser Nursery.

In 1953, when Henry died at age 94, the children took over the business. Cecilia died in 1955, and, after the death of Tony and Emil, the business was run by Herman, Edith, and Helen. When Edith died, Herman attempted to carry on alone, working in the fields in the daytime and filling orders at night. Mary Bresser Young, Herman's daughter, who had a family of her own, gave her father all the assistance she could during this time.

In 1980 the Bresser estate sold Bresser Nursery to Jack Theimer. Herman and his sister Helen retained five acres of the land on which they had built their home, and they now reside at 1501 North York.

CITIZENS NATIONAL BANK AND TRUST OF MUSKOGEE

Citizens National Bank and Trust of Muskogee was founded on Friday, April 13, 1926, by M. S. Martin, J. T. Griffin, L. H. Rooney, Carr Peterson, Tom F. King, and H. C. Bain with an original capital stock of $100,000 and a paid-in surplus of $20,000.

Although Friday the 13th has connotations of bad luck for many people, it proved a day of good fortune for Citizens; 94 customers had deposited $112,842.19 at the close of the first day of business.

The bank's original home at 325 West Broadway was adequate for the first 25 years, but by the early 1950s growth and expansion of the bank's physical facilities would begin and last through much of the 1960s. In May of 1951 a parking lot behind the bank was added. Drive-in facilities behind the bank were added in August of 1954, and the following year the parking lot was extended. In 1965 Citizens purchased the Modern Clothiers Building adjoining the main bank building, and its floor space was doubled in 1972 when it took possession of and expanded into what had been the Clothiers building after a complete renovation. Citizens' mini-bank, started in 1969, was completed the following year.

Past presidents of Citizens include: M. A. Martin, 1926-1930; L. H. Rooney, 1930-1936; J. T. Griffin, 1936-1940; L. F. Rooney, 1944-1960; Thomas Tarpley, 1960-1972; Justin W. Campbell (who came to work for the bank in July of 1939 as a $125-a-month bookkeeper), 1972-1978; and Lake Moore, III, who assumed the presidency in 1978 and holds that position today.

Beginning with 10 employees, Citizens today has 81 full-time employees, some of whom have served at the bank for many years:

Old and new homes of Citizens National Bank.

for example, Campbell, who serves as Chairman of the Board today, and Jess M. Ross, who came to Citizens in January of 1938 as a teller at $125 a month and retired in January of 1980 after serving 42 years at the bank.

From 94 first-day depositors, Citizens has grown to 7400 depositors with total assets in excess of $80 million and capital of $8,777,000.

Officers of Citizens, today a full-service bank, include: Justin W. Campbell, Chairman of the Board; Lake Moore, III, President and Chief Executive Officer; Buford D. Groom, Senior Vice President; Richard C. Haugland, David F. Jones, L. F. Rooney, III, Vice Presidents; Albert R. Hurley, Vice President and Cashier; Melvin R. Camp, Jr., Vice President and Trust Officer; Evelyn H. Simpson, Vice President and Administrative Assistant; Barbara L. Synar, Vice President, Customer Services; John L. Cohea, Vice President, Business Development; Dale L. Asher, Vernon Sisson, John L. Pannell, Vice Presidents, Installment Loans; Terry Smethers, Larry Scott, As-

sistant Vice Presidents; Agnes L. Roberts, Operations Officer; Doris Kuykendall, Wanda Archibald, Customer Service Officers; and Joyce Pierce, Credit Officer.

Directors of the bank are: J. E. Arnold, Investments; James C. Buchanan, III, Investments; William A. Buckley, Griffin Grocery Company; Justin W. Campbell, Chairman of the Board; John T. Griffin, Griffin Grocery Company; Buford D. Groom, Senior Vice President; Richard C. Haugland, Vice President; Lake Moore, III, President; Robert L. Motter, Jr., Motter Bookbinding; L. F. Rooney, III, Manhattan Construction Company; and James R. Voss, Fullerton Electric Supply, Inc.

Citizens saw many changes in 1981: the formation of a one-bank holding company, Citizens Dimension Bancorp, Inc.; formation of plans for a new main bank plant; and there will be more changes for Citizens in the future. However, one thing will not change—Citizens' role not only as a "Builder of Greater Muskogee," but also its role as a leader in the partnership it has had with Muskogee for 56 years.

COBURN RANCH

Although all business ventures O.W. Coburn undertook were done with one purpose in mind—making money—the C-Rocket Ranch began as a weekend retreat and a place of fun for the Coburns.

O. W. began purchasing land, at first in 40-acre tracts, in 1955. Five years later he and his brother John bought 34 head of commercial cattle at the Muskogee Stockyards to put on 160 acres south of Muskogee. In 1962 they began serious discussions as to what type of cattle they should stock on the ranch instead of having different breeds on this 160-acre tract.

They decided on Charolais and bought seven head from a rancher named Montgomery. That same year of 1962 O. W. purchased another 160 acres seven miles west of town. This ranch was known locally as the "Round Barn Ranch" because of the unusual round barn on the property. The Charolais were moved to this location, and all other commercial breeds were sold.

In the mid-1960s O. W. bought the 200-acre Brazil Ranch located just one mile west of the Round Barn Ranch, and more Charolais were added. The Coburn brothers' partnership continued until a year later when O. W. sold the Brazil property to John, who then renamed it the "J. R." for his son John Robert. The brothers continued buying Charolais to stock their individual ranches when these cattle were available.

At approximately the same time the brothers dissolved their joint ranching venture, O. W. purchased 1500 acres near the Jamesville "Y" from Jack Summers. Ranching now became a serious business for him. In the November 15, 1970, issue of Oklahoma Ranch and Farm World, a reporter stated that "when Coburn purchased the Summers Ranch, he proceeded to run it on a business basis as he had learned to do with his manufacturing concern. And it has paid off."

O. W. continued to add acreage until today the ranch totals about 7000 acres, and the Charolais herd has constantly been improved. In 1973 he bought 20 to 25 of the finest Charolais in America from Nelson Bunker Hunt. Although the Coburn cattle previously had been registered, this purchase upgraded the C-Rocket blood-line until it was the best in the United States.

Although O. W. is definitely in the ranching business to make money, not everything at the ranch has been done for profit. In 1977 he bought a herd of buffalo consisting of 50 cows and three bulls; these he kept near the front of the ranch. At the same time he purchased three llamas, two females and a male. Since then he has added several head of deer, burros, sheep, and pheasants. According to John, this is almost a small zoo. When asked why he bought such animals, O. W. answered that he believes "We should remember our American heritage."

The buffalo no longer are at the ranch. Because they were difficult to keep in an enclosed area and, when they escaped, posed a hazard to passing motorists, he sold them to a rancher in Kansas. The other animals, as well as his bloodline of Charolais, which attracts buyers and cattlemen from around the world, still make the C-Rocket Ranch a favorite stop for school children throughout the area and for all visitors to northeastern Oklahoma.

Coburn Autrichien No. 22.

COLE GRAIN COMPANY

Muskogee's Cole Grain Company, one of the most fully automated feed plants in the United States, began with one deteriorated head house in 1940. Since 1911 Howard V. Cole had owned and operated two grain elevators, one in Welch and the other in Bluejacket, Oklahoma. Then in 1939, when tornadoes destroyed both elevators, he and his son, Joy D., born in Elgin in 1903, decided to relocate. They drove to Muskogee and saw the possibilities for a grain elevator near the rich farmland in the Three Forks area.

Joy contacted the Fort Worth owner of the old grain elevator at 919 South Cherokee and arranged to buy it. He, his wife Olivia, and their two children (Sam, then three, and Mary Patricia, just a baby) moved to Muskogee in 1940.

According to Olivia, Cole Grain Company started "literally from nothing." Every belt, bucket, and window had to be replaced in the old elevator, and even the one-room office near it had to be rebuilt. Because corn was the principal crop in the area at that time, the first purchase by the fledgling company was a corn sheller and dryer (the dryer was the first in northeastern Oklahoma).

In 1954, changing with the times, Cole Grain switched to processing dehydrated alfalfa. A large drum for the dryer was installed at the plant. That same year Joy formed a partnership and bought the Choska Alfalfa Mill in Choska Bottom. Business increased to the point that a few years later the dryer was too small, and a new one was installed at the Choska plant. In 1950, thanks to a loan arranged through Louis Duncan and the Commercial Bank, Cole purchased the plant at Choska from his partners.

In 1954 storage bins capable of holding 325,000 bushels of grain were added to the growing plant in Muskogee. Six years later two large French Presses for processing soy beans into meal and oil were installed, and in 1963 a push button feed mill was added and a much-needed new office building was constructed. Cole Grain stopped processing alfalfa in Muskogee during the 1960s because the plant was too small to be profitable.

Donald R. Cole, the youngest son, returned from Viet Nam and joined the company in 1971. Born on April 1, 1946, Don attended local schools in Muskogee, then received his degree in business and economics from the University of Oklahoma. He also had taken four years of military science courses, and afterward he served with the armed forces at San Antonio and in Viet Nam north of Saigon in the administrative department of a military hospital. He and his wife Janie have four children, three daughters and a son. Today Don is vice president and general manager of the company.

Although cattle feed has been—and still is—the principal product manufactured at Cole Grain, a new plant and machinery for manufacturing dog food was installed in 1976. At first this was packaged only under Cole Grain's label, "Happy Hound," but now the firm processes dog food for several companies. In 1980 a second warehouse for pet food was built. This not only houses the machinery for producing dog food but also a cat food under Cole's "Contented Kitty" label, fish food, and other pet foods. Feeds for cattle, horses, and chickens are still packaged in the main plant.

Across the years Joy, who is president of the firm, has added to, remodeled, and invented devices for the machinery at Cole Grain to make the plant safer and more productive—with less work and risk for his employees.

Still growing, Cole Grain currently has plans for the addition of storage facilities for another 200,000 bushels in addition to the more than 100 bins it already has in place.

COMMERCIAL BANK AND TRUST COMPANY

Shanties forming early downtown Muskogee in the 1890s included a one-room frame structure on the east side of Main Street where John H. Dill opened the door to banking customers under the name "The Commercial Bank." Dill began with $700 and a strong belief in the future of Indian Territory. With steady growth and the need for expansion, the bank moved several times, once to the "English Block" occupying the northwest corner of Broadway and Main streets.

D. N. Fink was named president of Commercial in 1911 and served as a leading contributor to the city's growth and stability. In 1912 Commercial moved into the new Muskogee skyscraper, the Barnes Building, with its spacious lobby. Following a merger with the Exchange National Bank, Commercial moved into the Flynn-Ames Building, which became the Commercial National Building at Third and Broadway. A change of ownership occurred in 1926 when C. F. Lynde and J. F. Darby purchased a controlling interest in the institution. The reorganization brought in a gentleman as president who became the bedrock of Commercial.

Louis W. Duncan planted the seeds of an oak with his skills of leadership. He steered the bank through the Great Depression with quiet strength and courage. In fact, Commercial was one of the first institutions to reopen at the earliest date permitted after the "bank holiday" was decreed in 1933. During World War II Commercial even had a legal branch bank (unheard of in Oklahoma) at nearby Camp Gruber. Duncan proudly watched as the bank and Muskogee settled into a period of steady growth and stability. He, along with directors and officers like Bert O. Baker and Morton Woods, Jr., were building the bank's foundation for the future.

In 1966 Commercial Bank closed the year with $24,852,000 in total assets and a new president. Bert Baker took over the reins and quickly led the bank through a complete renovation of the building, followed by the formation of Commercial Landmark Corporation, one of the first bank holding companies in Oklahoma. By 1971 Commercial, based originally on $700 in assets, had become the largest bank in Muskogee. Under Baker's leadership, Commercial has almost doubled its assets every five years, finishing 1981 at more than $150 million.

During the 1970s innovative management by Commercial brought ideas into reality with programs like data processing, automatic teller machines, and extended banking hours.

In addition, Commercial Bank has one of Oklahoma's outstanding art and antique collections, open to the public during banking hours.

Directors of Commercial Bank and Trust Company are: Bert O. Baker, Chairman of the Board; Jerry D. Baker, President; Dave L. Blakeburn, Senior Vice President; R. P. Campbell; D. Richard Clark; James M. Coburn; Donald R. Cole; Thurman Curtsinger; Louis W. Duncan, Chairman Emeritus and Honorary Director; A. G. Hayes; Lee Howser; Austin Kenyon; Robert L. Morhart, President, Commercial Landmark; Richard D. Newkirk; W. H. Pool; William H. Ricketts; Donald Rex Robertson; W. E. Rowsey, Jr.; Paul J. Shierl; Edmund Synar; Joe Teaff; Taft Welch; and Morton Woods, Jr., Executive Vice President.

COUSINS SHOES

Cousins Shoes is one of the oldest continuing businesses in downtown Muskogee. Located at 306 West Broadway, it first opened its doors in 1917 as a shoe repair shop, and when Floyd and Mildred Cousins bought the shop on May 13, 1940, they continued the shoe repair tradition.

At the time of the purchase, Floyd, who had moved to Muskogee with his family in 1913 from Sapulpa, was no stranger to the shoe repair business. In 1920 he started in shoe repair as a delivery boy for a shop located at 421 West Okmulgee. In addition to deliveries, Floyd buttoned and laced high topped shoes. Five years later, in 1925, when Floyd was 19 years old, he bought the shop for $400 and then sold it in 1927 to return to school. He enrolled at the University of Oklahoma, but dropped out a year and a half later because, according to him, he was not "cut out for school."

After working and traveling around the country for the next several years, Floyd returned to Oklahoma and in 1936 met and married Mildred Barrick, who was attending school in Stillwater at the time. The Cousins were on their way to Albuquerque, New Mexico, in 1940 when they stopped for a visit in Muskogee and bought the shoe repair shop.

From 1942 through 1946 the shoe repair business boomed. The Cousins employed eight full-time repairmen to assist Floyd. In addition to shoe repair, the Cousins offered a complete shoe shine service, often employing six shoe shine boys at the same time to accommodate the hundreds of servicemen who came to Muskogee from Camp Gruber during the war years.

Between 1948 and 1962 Cousins' repaired shoes were entered in the National Repair Contest five times—and never placed below 16th or above 6th in the competition. In 1950 and again in 1952 the Cousins were awarded a gold-plated hammer and awl. Mildred had these mounted and gave one to each of their children, Joel, of Muskogee, and Sally Cousins Elliot, of Washington, D.C. In addition, the Cousins have won five blue ribbons in national competition for their work.

In the years that followed, because of the unavailability of reliable shoe repairmen, the Cousins were unable to continue the shoe repair business on a full-time basis. In the early 1950s they remodeled the store in a Western motif, and throughout the 1950s and 1960s carried a full line of Western and Indian wear, as well as Indian arts and crafts. During this decade the Cousins enjoyed a flourishing tourist trade.

In 1955, in addition to part-time shoe repair and Western wear, Floyd began filling prescriptions for orthopedic shoes. He was able to do this only after passing an extensive written examination and having been recommended by two orthopedic surgeons. In the early 1960s Cousins gave up the shoe repair and Western wear business altogether.

In 1970 the name was changed to "Cousins Shoes, Inc.," and so it remains today. In addition to filling orthopedic prescriptions for five doctors, Floyd is registered to sell and make all parts of orthopedic shoes, although most of the time he makes the mold, cuts the pattern, and contracts the actual shoe building.

Cousins Shoes' customers come from all over the United States, but the majority are local. Some are old customers who have moved away but still return to Cousins for their shoes; others are customers who have heard of Cousins' expertise in orthopedic shoes and travel hundreds of miles for the proper-fitting shoe the Cousins require.

Styled shoes no longer are stocked by Cousins Shoes. Today only reinforced, corrective shoes are found on the shelves that line the walls of the store. Floyd is semi-retired, but Mildred, who has worked with Floyd all these years, still works a regular eight-hour day. Neither wants to retire competely until they find someone to take over Cousins Shoes who will continue in the tradition of community service that this shoe shop has given for more than 65 years—42 of them given by Floyd and Mildred Cousins.

THE CRUCIFIXION

Since time began, all forms of communication have been used to share the Word of God with the entire world—Billy Graham has a dynamic speaking ability, Mahalia Jackson an incomparable song, and Muskogee's Gloria Schumann a paint brush and canvas.

As partial fulfillment of a vow she made two years prior to her husband's death in 1956, Gloria has created in oil a unique, moving interpretation of the Crucifixion of Christ. It is unique because the viewer does not look up into the face of the Christ figure, as most crucifixion scenes are depicted, but instead stands at shoulder height behind the Christ figure and looks down into the faces of those who loved Him as well as those who nailed Him to the cross. It is moving because in the eyes of all those looking upward, in addition to the agony of watching Him die, is the faith and knowledge that only His body leaves them—never His spirit and love.

The Crucifixion is the first religious painting executed by Gloria, who was a well-known portrait artist before she moved to Muskogee in 1970. Several of her better-known portrait commissions were President-elect Richard M. Nixon's inaugural portrait, two paitings of Martha Mitchell in her inaugural gown, and one of Attorney General John Mitchell.

The Crucifixion is the result of three years of dedicated work, plus almost two years of extensive Bible study before she began the 6 by 7 foot painting. The Bible study continues today.

Gloria recalls that, when she came to Muskogee in 1970, she learned to love the people of the city and of the state of Oklahoma with its "wall to wall sky." She now resides and paints in her specially designed studio-home in Honor Heights Park. Her home is built in the shape of a cross (when viewed from above).

All models in the Crucifixion scene, a painting which Gloria says is "for the people, of the people, and by the people" of Muskogee, are her friends and neighbors who were introduced to her by Mrs. Martha Griffin. Gloria extends her love and gratitude to those who made this work a reality: the Christ figure, Chuck Fullenwilder; Mary, wife of Clopas, Ann Kuykendall; John, the disciple, Paul Edward Rowsey, III; Mary, Mother of Christ, Martha Watson Griffin; Bartimaeus, Mark Hine; Martha of Bethany, Joan Fite; Mary of Bethany, Marianne Rowsey; Young nobleman, Nick Fuller; Mary Magdalene, Suzan Bauman Hays; Salome, Connie Lynde Haugland; Mourner, Lou Hays; Mourner, Beverly Stevenson; Lazarus, Bernie Susman, Jr.; Longinus, the Centurion, Brad Hoops; Shepherd, John Reynolds; Barabbas, Jim Warren; Joseph of Arimathaea, Bill Fitzgerald; Joanna, wife of Chuza, Dessa Kuykendall; Peter, David Stevenson; Andrew, Steven Waters; James, Gary Kuykendall.

Reference "Slides of Israel" were furnished by Laurel N. Childers. Reference books were used from Jim Gibson, *Life of Christ*, by Giovanni Papini, and Fulton Owsler's *Greatest Story Ever Told*. Gloria wishes to thank the Howard Perry Ranch, Al Cheeseman, Walker Christain, Margaret Procter, Mrs. Horace McReynolds, and Lillian Lange Barton.

The artist also would like to acknowledge the help and teaching over the past 10 years by her Bible teacher, Lorraine Taylor Childers.

"The Crucifixion"
by Gloria Schumann.

FEDERAL COURT COMES TO MUSKOGEE

On April 1, 1889, "Hear ye! Hear ye!" resounded in the small crowded frame Knights of Phythias Hall in Muskogee, and the first U. S. District Court in the Indian Territory was in session. The coming of the court further girded Muskogee's base for substantial growth.

Until then, Indian Nation courts had jurisdiction over their citizens, with non-Indians coming under federal courts outside the Territory. Non-citizens in the Creek and Cherokee Nations were subject to the court at Fort Smith, Arkansas.

As the non-Indian population grew, however, law enforcement became unmanageable. Realizing the need, Congress on March 1, 1889, passed an act establishing a federal court for the Indian Territory. Due to the efforts of Pleasant Porter, the court was located at Muskogee.

James N. Shackleford of Indiana was the first judge, presiding in the temporary quarters. On June 24 the cornerstone was laid for a permanent court building on Second Street, the side street becoming Court Street. Court convened there until the stone federal structure was built on Fifth Street in 1912.

In 1895 the Indian Territory was divided into three federal court districts, later four, and the number of judges increased accordingly. In 1897 Judge John R. Thomas came to Muskogee as the first federal judge-at-large to serve all districts as needed.

Judges succeeding James Shackleford at Muskogee were William M. Springer, 1895; Charles W. Raymond, 1901; Louis Sulzbacher, 1904; and William R. Lawrence, 1905.

At statehood the Muskogee court became the U. S. District

On April 1, 1889, the federal court was opened in Muskogee by: (front row, L. to R.) Judge James M. Shackleford and Court Clerk William Nelson; (back row, L. to R.) Marshal Thomas B. Needles and District Attorney Zachary T. Walrond.

Court for the Eastern District of Oklahoma. Succeeding judges were Ralph E. Campbell, 1907; Robert L. Williams, 1919; Eugene Rice, 1937; Edwin Langley, 1965; Joseph W. Morris, 1974; and Frank H. Seay, 1979. Bower Broaddus, a Muskogee attorney, became a roving judge in 1940, and Luther Bohanon, a native Muskogeean, became one in 1961.

Muskogee has ever had a distinguished bar. In the Chal Wheeler Law Library hang pictures of members through the years. William Howard Taft, when Chief Justice of the U. S. Supreme Court, once named the 12 lawyers who had made the best appearances before the U. S. Supreme Court. Of the 12, two were Nathan A. Gibson and George S. Ramsey of Muskogee. Under Woodrow Wilson, Preston C. West of Muskogee served as Assistant Attorney General of the United States.

In some Muskogee families, a legal career was traditional. Three

generation families are: E. Ross Jones, Preston W. Jones, and Preston W. Jones, Jr.; and Archibald Bonds, A. Camp Bonds, and A. Camp Bonds, Jr. Firms with father-and-sons include: Ed Edmondson, Drew Edmondson, and James E. Edmondson; and Andrew Wilcoxen, Drew Wilcoxen, and James Wilcoxen. Father-and-son firms include: Jesse Watts and Owen J. Watts; Malcolm E. Rosser and Malcolm E. Rosser, Jr.; Benjamin Martin and Richard Martin; Julian B. Fite and Julian K. Fite; John W. Porter and John W. Porter, Jr.; and R. P. de Graffenried and Mosley de Graffenried.

Fathers and sons practicing but not together include Norman Haskell and Charles N. Haskell, II; Cleon A. Summers and Hardy Summers; Charles Wheeler and Chal Wheeler; J. R. Settle and Bill Settle; and Chester Norman and Mike Norman. Firms consisting of brothers include Ed Edmondson and J. Howard Edmondson; Earl Boyd Pierce and Ray M. Pierce; Enloe Vernor and Vilas Vernor; Claude E. Garrett and Douglas C. Garrett; and Eck E., Ed K., and Arthur Brooks. James D. Gibson and John Gibson, brothers, were members of the firm Gotwals, Gibson, Killey, and Gibson.

Officials appointed or elected from the Muskogee Bar have included two U. S. Senators; two Congressmen; a Governor; Supreme, District, County, and City judges; Federal Commissioners; presidents of the Oklahoma Bar Association; and many state, county, and city officers.

After the state bar examinations are held each year, young lawyers newly admitted to practice arrive to join the Muskogee Bar Association.

The Muskogee Court continues in session.

FIRST NATIONAL BANK AND TRUST COMPANY OF MUSKOGEE

The First originally was in the Severs Block.

The present home of the First.

The oldest bank in Oklahoma—the First National Bank and Trust Company of Muskogee—was organized on June 7, 1890, after more than a year of negotiations begun by Robert L. Owen, C. E. Foley, and other citizens of the frontier city of Muskogee.

The bank's first Board of Directors consisted of Robert L. Owen, President, A. W. Robb, T. B. Needles, F. B. Severs, P. J. Byrne, C. W. Turner, and Leo Bennett, all of Muskogee; H. W. Salmon, Clinton, Missouri; W. O. Cox, Kansas City, Missouri; C. E. Foley, Eufaula; J. E. Reynolds, South McAlester; and John Adams, Parsons, Kansas.

After the charter was approved, the bank opened for business on April 22, 1890, with a capital structure of $100,000 at its first location in the Severs block building on the southeast corner of Second Street and Broadway. In 1908 the City National Bank was absorbed, further increasing the size and enlarging the field of services of First National.

On March 1, 1913, First National moved into a newly purchased three-story building at 202 West Broadway. Several years later the top floor of the building was removed, making the structure the two stories it is today.

By 1919 the capital structure had increased to $675,000. Ten years later, in 1929, the bank had undergone two name changes, the first near the turn of the century when the spelling of "Muscogee" was changed, and the second in 1929 when "and Trust Company" was added because of the growth of the bank's trust department.

Because of able management and the support of the community, the bank continued its pattern of steady growth. By 1940 the capital had reached $858,000, and in the early 1950s construction of additional parking facilities and drive-through windows under the main offices of the bank were completed.

Continuing to grow and give better services to customers, the First National on August 5, 1964, completed a new four-level parking facility across Second Street from the main offices; 125 cars, with maximum ingress and egress, can be parked, and another 50 can be parked in case of heavy traffic. In the late 1970s, 10 drive-through windows were installed between Second and Third streets on Dennison.

Presidents of First National Bank include H. H. Ogden, Harry W. Gibson, Jr., Ora W. Lamb, William Kaad, and H. E. Leonard, the current President.

Today's Directors are: Andy Anderson, H. E. Anderson Company; William H. Boies, Royal Casket Company; Edward Buddrus, Acme Engineering Company; Cecil J. Graham, Muskoge Iron Works; Ronald J. Grubb, Chairman of the Board; A. B. Hensley, Hensley-Nichols Insurance Agency; H. E. Leonard, President and Trust Officer; Michael S. Leonard, Executive Vice President, Charles Pearson, farming; James P. Rowsey, City Chevrolet Company; Frank Smith, Zapata Industries, Inc.; Robert B. Thompson, Oklahoma Rig and Supply Company, Inc.; Jack H. Walker, W. P. Milling Company, Inc.; William S. Warner, Jr., Warner Properties; and Robert N. Yaffe, Yaffe Iron and Metal Company, Inc.

Today, after 92 years of continuous service to Muskogee and the surrounding area, current assets of First National Bank and Trust Company are $89.5 million and capital accounts stand at $7 million.

DR. EDWARD HALSELL FITE

Dr. Edward Halsell Fite was the son of Dr. Francis Bartow Fite, one of the prominent pioneer physicians in northeastern Oklahoma. Dr. Bartow Fite was the first surgeon in Indian Territory and established the first hospital, St. Mary's Sanitarium, later known as Martha Robb Hospital, in what now is Oklahoma. He also served two terms as mayor of the city of Muskogee.

Edward Halsell Fite, the fourth of five children, was born on December 27, 1898, in Muskogee, I.T. Educated in Muskogee elementary schools, he graduated from Shattuck Military Academy at Faribault, Minnesota, where he was the battalion commander.

At the outbreak of World War I, he enlisted in the army and was stationed at Camp Lee, Virginia, where he was in officers' training when the conflict ended. He then attended the University of Virginia, where he earned his bachelor of science and his doctor of medicine degrees.

Dr. Fite interned at the University of Virginia and served his residency in Urology at Massachusetts General Hospital in Boston before returning to Muskogee to join his father and brother in the Fite Clinic. In 1924 he married Elizabeth Coleman Williams, daughter of Dr. and Mrs. J. Fulton Williams of Charlottesville, Virginia.

Dr. Edward Halsell Fite.

Dr. Fite was a staff member of both Muskogee General and Baptist hospitals, and served on the Muskogee City Council for eight years. He was a member of the International College of Surgeons, the American College of Surgeons, the American Medical Association, the American Urological Association, the South Central Section of the American Urological Association (past president), the Oklahoma Urological Society (past president), and numerous other medical organizations.

Dr. Fite died on October 17, 1973, after more than 50 years of medical service. But the Fite tradition of medicine did not end, for it is being carried on by his sons, Dr. Edward Halsell Fite, Jr., and Dr. Fulton Williams Fite.

Dr. Edward Halsell Fite, Jr., received his medical degree from the University of Virginia, where he also completed his internship and his residency in Urology. He is a navy veteran of both World War II and the Korean Conflict and is now senior partner in the Muskogee Urological Clinic.

Dr. Fulton Williams Fite also attended the University of Virginia, earning his bachelor of arts, master's, and doctor of medicine degrees. He trained further in the United States Air Force, receiving specialty training in surgery and otolaryngology. He retired from the Air Force in 1977 as a full colonel and now is in the private practice of otolaryngology in Muskogee.

Coleman Bartow Fite, a third son, broke tradition and chose a different career, graduating from the University of Oklahoma in 1952 with a degree in geology. Since graduation, he has been active in the oil industry, farming, and ranching, and now is president of Fite-Reynolds Real Estate Company. Carrying on the family involvement in community affairs, he now is serving his third term as mayor of the city of Muskogee.

FITE HOME

The Francis Bartow Fite home at 16th Street and Emporia Avenue is a landmark and a symbol of Muskogee's proud and fascinating history. The foundation was laid in 1906, but the house was not completed until December of 1907 because of the difficulty involved in hauling the quarry-faced Carthage stone (of which the entire house is built) from Carthage, Missouri. The cost of the house, less the interior decorating had risen to $32,000 by the time the Fite family had their first meal in their new home—Christmas dinner.

Francis Bartow Fite, born and raised in Georgia, came to Indian Territory in 1883 to open and operate a pharmacy for his half-brother, James Thompson, who already was practicing medicine in Tahlequah. Fite operated the pharmacy for a while and then was hired by the Cherokee Nation to teach elementary school. He taught only long enough to save the money to return to Georgia and study medicine. After finishing medical school, Dr. Bartow Fite returned to Tahlequah and entered practice with Thompson.

Within a few years, however, he moved to Muskogee and then to New York to intern at the New York Poly Clinic, after which he re-turned to Muskogee to become the first surgeon in Indian Territory. Later Dr. Bartow Fite would start the first hospital in Indian Territory, one of the forerunners of today's Muskogee General Hospital.

In 1889 Dr. Bartow Fite married Julia Patton. The Pattons also were from Georgia and had moved to Vinita where they operated a mercantile business after the Civil War.

The Fites had five children: William Patton, the oldest; F. Bartow; Edward Halsell; and the two youngest, and only surviving Fite children, a daughter, Frances, and another son, Julian.

After the death of Dr. Bartow Fite and Julia in 1940 and 1945 respectively, the home was remodeled into the Fite Clinic under Drs. Pat and Halsell Fite. The other three Fite children donated their interest in the home to the Fite Clinic. Today the Fite home, which from the beginning has housed those serving the medical needs of the people of Muskogee, continues that tradition. It is the home of Dr. David R. Watson's Pediatric Clinic.

Julian Fite has served the Muskogee community as prestigiously as the other members of his family, although in a different profession. He was born in Muskogee on September 30, 1906, attended local el-ementary schools, high school at Shattuck Military Academy in Faribault, Minnesota, and obtained his law degree from the University of Virginia in 1931. After his return to Muskogee, he was admitted to the Oklahoma Bar Association in 1932 and married Helen Kroh in 1935.

Julian opened his law practice with a partner, Bower Broaddus. The partnership was dissolved when Broaddus was appointed a federal judge. Julian joined the Air Force in 1940 and, after serving almost four years as Judge Advocate, returned to Muskogee and private practice. He was appointed City Attorney and then general attorney for the First National Bank in 1948. In the early 1950s he again formed a law partnership (with Carl Robinson and Hardy Summers), but disolved the partnership and retired in the early 1960s because of illness.

Today Julian, who has served on the Board of Governors and as a trustee for the Oklahoma Bar Association, has returned to active practice. He takes only a few interesting cases. Helen manages the couple's real estate business, the Indian Capital Agency. Frances Ambuster, Julian's sister, lives, since the death of her husband Hubert, with her daughter in Dallas.

FIVE CIVILIZED TRIBES MUSEUM

The Museum Building as it looks today.

Opening its doors in April of 1956 with only three paintings, The Five Civilized Tribes Museum has grown until today it has more than 300 of the finest paintings of the Five Tribes in its collection. Its wood and bronze sculptures, numbering almost 300, include some of the rarest pieces yet created by members of the Five Tribes, and its authentic artifacts visually tell the story of the Five Tribes. All are on permanent display at the Museum.

Located in the old Union Agency building on Agency Hill in Honor Heights Park, the building itself is as much a part of the proud history and tradition of the Five Tribes as the treasures found within. The Union Agency was the first building erected by the United States government to house the superintendency of the Five Tribes, but was used for this purpose for only a short time. Since that summer day of August 18, 1875, when the cornerstone was laid, however, the native stone structure has stood as a steadfast symbol of the Five Civilized Tribes.

Although the offices of the superintendency were moved from the Union Agency down the hill to be near the Katy Railroad, the building remained in the possession of the Creek Nation until 1909 when ownership was conveyed to the City of Muskogee to be used for park purposes.

In 1944 Muskogee gave the agency and five and one-half acres of land to the government to augment the facilities of the Veterans Hospital, but the government never put the building to use.

Ten years later, in 1954, the Da-Co-Tah Indian Club of Muskogee, with a museum in mind, sponsored House Bill 8983 petitioning the return of the building to the city. United States Representative Ed Edmondson (D-Okla.) of Muskogee introduced the Bill in Congress, and after its passage it was signed on July 28, 1954, by President Dwight D. Eisenhower. The Five Civilized Tribes Museum was incorporated on November 19, 1955, under the laws of the State of Oklahoma.

Over the next several years the citizens of Muskogee raised $94,000 to restore the building to its original state with no help from federal, state, or city governments. Even children sold pop bottles so their names might be included on the restoration list.

In 1966 when the Museum officially opened, Peggy Denton was named director. Today she still holds that position and is an invaluable part of the Museum.

The art gallery is a nationally recognized Indian art gallery and is the only gallery in the world devoted exclusively to traditional Indian art. Hanging in the gallery is one of the largest and most complete collections of the work of the late Jerome Tiger, noted Creek-Seminole artist. In addition to his paintings, the Museum also has Tiger's nationally known sculpture, a life-size stickball player (now cast in bronze), along with three of the few existing small sculptures Tiger created.

The Museum also has one of the largest collections of sculptures of Willard Stone, a Cherokee, considered by many critics to be the greatest living Indian wood sculptor in the world, as well as many works by the noted bronzer, St. Clair Homer, a Choctaw-Chickasaw. The Museum Library contains more than 3500 rare books and original documents which, although never checked out, are available to visitors.

The Five Civilized Tribes Museum is the only organization in the United States whose sole purpose since its conception has been to collect, preserve, display, and make available to visitors and researchers the continuous and full histories of the Cherokees, Creeks, Seminoles, Choctaws, and Chickasaws—the Five Civilized Tribes—a proud people who have contributed greatly to the state and nation.

JUDGE JOHN R. THOMAS AND GRANT AND CAROLEYN FOREMAN HOME

The original Thomas home. Right: Note the porch was enclosed.

John R. Thomas, an Illinois attorney and member of the U. S. House of Representatives from 1879 to 1889, where his accomplishments earned him the title of father of the modern U. S. Navy, came to Muskogee in 1897 to serve a term as Federal Judge at large of Indian Territory. He remained in Muskogee the rest of his life.

In May of 1898, after his arrival in Muskogee, his daughter Carolyn came to live with him at the Adams Hotel. According to those who knew her, she enjoyed telling people she spent her first day in Muskogee in court attending the trial of Al Jennings, an outlaw.

Carolyn Thomas was born in Illinois, and after the death of her mother, when Carolyn was eight years old, she attended school in Washington, D. C., Monticello Seminary in Godfrey, Illinois, and abroad. After moving to Muskogee, she quickly formed lasting friendships with Indian families and newcomers.

After the Adams Hotel burned in 1899, Judge Thomas purchased a tract of Turner-Porter prairie land which later would be known as 1419 West Okmulgee. Here he built his home, a home that mirrors Muskogee life from 1899 to 1967.

Judge Thomas was often vis-ited by his son, John R. Thomas, Junior, and in 1898, when the judge recruited men for a regiment of Rough Riders to go to Cuba, his son went as First Lieutenant of Troop L. John R., Jr., would have an outstanding military and diplomatic career.

In 1899 a young man named Grant Foreman came to Muskogee as law clerk to the Dawes Commission. Born in Illinois, he had graduated from the University of Michigan and practiced law briefly in Chicago before coming to Indian Territory. When the Dawes Commission work terminated in 1904, he joined Judge Thomas in his law practice. The following year he and Carolyn Thomas were married in the home of the bride, the residence which became their home.

Carolyn and Grant Foreman.

Judge Thomas was killed in a prison riot in 1914 when he went to McAlester to interview a client. Soon afterward, Foreman retired from law practice to write Indian and Southwestern history. From 1920 until his death in 1953, he wrote 15 books and edited four, in addition to publishing many articles.

The Foremans traveled extensively both for research and pleasure. At home they participated in civic and social affairs in addition to their heavy schedule of writing.

After Foreman's death, Thomas J. Pressley, first employed by Foreman in 1916, continued in service at the home. He remains there today.

In 1954 Carolyn Foreman attended the dedication of Muskogee's Grant Foreman School, so named at the suggestion of Miss Nettie Wheeler.

Mrs. Foreman died in 1967. Her will named her niece Mrs. William Biglow Nergaard (*nee* Hughberta Thomas) her heir. Mrs. Neergaard presented the Foreman home to the Oklahoma Historical Society. Today the home is open free to the public so that all who enter may take a step back into Muskogee's past.

GRIFFIN GROCERY

On October 1, 1908, J. T. and Charley Griffin opened the doors of a small rented storeroom in McAlester, Oklahoma, complete with a second-hand desk, a typewriter, some items discarded by other businesses, shipping containers for chairs, and unlimited faith. Within two years the newly formed Griffin Grocery, with an original investment of $10,000, had grown to the point that additional offices and warehouse facilities were needed. Griffin Grocery, handling only fresh produce, extended north to Muskogee and Miami, west to Okmulgee, and east to Fort Smith, Arkansas. In 1911 the firm was incorporated as Griffin Grocery.

Charley Griffin, co-founder of the company, passed away in 1915. His family remained associated with the company for many years. In 1917 Griffin Grocery began manufacturing goods to distribute under the Griffin label, and the following January the first shipment of high-grade Griffin Coffee left the plant.

By 1923 Griffin Grocery was firmly committed to the "manufacturing wholesaler" concept and recognized the need for a more central location. By 1925 a large, three-story processing plant and administrative office building had been constructed in Muskogee. By 1928 Griffin Grocery had grown from a business of less than $100,000 in sales during its first year to a $5 million sales corporation.

The decade of the 1930s, depression years that brought failure and bankruptcy to businesses across the United States, in contrast was a decade of rapid expansion for Griffin Grocery. In this decade the company engaged in the manufacturing of a great variety of

Left: J. T. Griffin.

products. English peas and corn were canned for a time; baking powder, under the Hi-Lo and Griffin labels, was a big item; salad dressing was added in 1935; and Griffin Waffle Syrup became the leading product. In the early 1940s the wholesale division expanded its territory through the addition of a number of branches.

J. T. Griffin, founder of the company, died in September of 1944. On his death, control of Griffin Grocery passed to his daughter Marjory and her husband, James C. Leake, and to his son John T. Griffin.

During the 1950s the product line was consolidated into items which could be processed efficiently in Oklahoma, and the area of distribution was increased greatly. The company began to concentrate its efforts in its manufacturing division on table syrup, preserves and jellies, salad dressing, coconut, and mustard. The distribution area was enlarged to include much more territory.

In 1978 the wholesale operation of the company was consolidated in a large, modern warehouse in Van Buren, Arkansas, which serves a radius of 250 miles. This division of Griffin Grocery has enjoyed rapid growth since construction of the new warehouse.

Seventy-four years after its founding, Griffin Grocery is still in the produce business and, in fact, to a much greater extent than before. This division is growing rapidly. The food manufacturing and processing business has improved remarkably in the quality of its products and in the area of its distribution. The company thus has continued in essentially the same activities as when it first was created by J. T. Griffin in 1908.

HEARON STEEL

Had D. N. "Doc" and Marilyn Hearon realized their dreams, the Hearon Steel Company in all probability would not have been established. And even after Hearon Steel became a reality, it would not have been located in Muskogee had fate not intervened.

Doc had never thought of pursuing any career other than teaching and coaching. Marilyn had chosen nursing as her profession and was working toward that goal when she and Doc married in 1949. However, after receiving a teaching and coaching degree from the University of Oklahoma in 1955 and then serving two years in the armed forces, Doc realized he could not support his growing family on a teaching salary.

In 1958 he went to work for the Robberson Steel Company in Oklahoma City, but left that firm in 1965 to help organize the Frontier Steel Company in Muskogee. He remained with Frontier Steel as a junior partner until 1970 when he and others formed a partnership and founded Continental Steel of Sapulpa. The next year Doc bought out his partners and changed the name to The Hearon Steel Company.

Deciding to relocate in a larger, more industrialized area, the Hearons chose Tulsa as the logical place. In 1971 they applied for a loan from the Tulsa County Industrial Trust. It was here that fate stepped in, for the loan was denied. The Hearons were told that Hearon Steel would not generate enough money and jobs to warrant the loan. Thus the Hearons looked elsewhere—and found Muskogee.

A loan was applied for and quickly approved, and in May of 1972 the first building of Hearon Steel—the reinforcement plant—was completed at 2301 Anderson Road, its present site in Muskogee.

The following years were good for Hearon Steel. In 1977 the company was presented a plaque from Armco Steel for having purchased the largest amount of steel from the western division of Armco during the preceding 12 months—23 million pounds.

In 1979 a structural steel plant was built next to the reinforcement plant, and the following year a subsidiary reinforcement plant was opened in Tulsa. Today Hearon Steel has 25 full-time employees, 16 in Muskogee and nine in Tulsa. Also during the summer months, a four-man night crew is employed part-time in Muskogee.

Doc is president and general manager of the company and plant manager in Muskogee. Vicki, the oldest of the three Hearon children, is plant manager in Tulsa. Marilyn, who after numerous interruptions finally fulfilled the requirements for a nursing degree at Bacone College in 1972, accepted a "temporary" position at the Muskogee plant in 1973. Nine years later she still is in that temporary position.

Since the move to Muskogee, Hearon Steel has supplied fabricated reinforcement and structural steel to be used in the construction of the Metropolitan Building, Cities Services Building, the Williams Center, the 71st Street Bridge, Hardesty Building, the new terminal building at the Tulsa International Airport, and several other buildings in Tulsa.

Hearon Steel also furnished the steel used in the construction of the Veterans Administration offices, and delivered more than 20 million pounds of steel to the Fort Howard Paper Company in Muskogee.

New contracts include the delivery of three million pounds of steel needed for construction of the third coal-fired generating unit for the Grand River Dam Authority in Pryor and fabricated reinforcement and structural steel for the new parking facilities at Tulsa International Airport.

Doc and Marilyn have never regretted their move to Muskogee. They are showing their appreciation and support of this community by giving Muskogee the proud distinction of being the home since 1975 of the largest volume steel reinforcing fabricators in Oklahoma.

LEROY KERSHAW

Clara A. Harrison Kershaw.

A sketch by Mrs. Kershaw.

Leroy Kershaw.

Leroy Kershaw's interest in farms, other real estate, and cattle began long before he came to Indian Territory. He was raised on a farm near Elmwood, Illinois, and, even after entering the University of Illinois, he did not break with his agricultural past. He financed his education by waiting on tables and by selling books, ice cream freezers, nursery stock, and real estate after school and the summer months.

While in college, L. R. had organized a farm sales agency and wanted to bring prospective land buyers to Oklahoma. He contacted J. Fred Darby in Muskogee and got Darby's listings. However, despite Darby's urging that L. R. join him in business, L. R. chose to form a partnership with William J. Anicker and E. A. Hippen. Each man invested $3000, and they formed the Illinois Trust and Investment Company in Muskogee, as well as Farmers State Bank in Morris.

One of L. R.'s first land buys in Muskogee was a 120-acre farm. That 120-acre farm, at 48th Street and West Okmulgee, is known today as Kershaw Heights. In the late Teens he ran the water line from Broadway and Junction streets to 45th Street.

A few years after college L. R. moved to Muskogee and contin-

ued buying and selling farms. Some he kept and farmed himself, at one time owning 15 farms in as many counties. One of these was a 1500-acre spread located 10 miles south and two miles east of Muskogee. He stocked this spread with Aberdeen Angus cattle. Between 1912 and 1958 he showed his prize-winning cattle across the United States. On May 15, 1920, he sold an Aberdeen Angus bull for $40,000, the highest price recorded for this breed to that time.

In 1924 L. R. married Clara A. Harrison, who would become an accomplished and well-known artist in Muskogee. Five children were born to the Kershaws: Patricia Ann Montgomery, the oldest; Robert Eugene and Elizabeth Jane Kunkel, the first set of twins; and Jean Mary Boehm and Joan Mary Putnam, the second set of twins.

L. R. fought and won a battle to lower the price of natural gas to the consumer. This led him, a staunch Republican, to run for governor of Oklahoma in 1930. However, he dropped out of the race when it became obvious "Bill" Murray would carry the solidly Democratic primary.

Another of L. R.'s accomplish-

ments was getting Bermuda grass established in Oklahoma as a summer foliage. He did this by asking people who were trying to get rid of Bermuda to save it for him. He then would haul it to one of his farms and plant it. Today Bermuda is one of the best grazing grasses in eastern Oklahoma.

Beginning in 1926 and afterward, L. R. was appointed receiver of 13 banks by the Comptroller of Currency. These banks, in Oklahoma, Arkansas, and Kansas, had become insolvent because of the depression. L. R. paid 96 to 106 percent of the depositors' accounts.

Kershaw developments in Muskogee include Kershaw Heights Addition, Kershaw Acres, Kershaw Drive Addition, Kershaw Circle Addition, and Home Acres I and II.

L. R. retired from active development to manage his varied holdings, dying at age 88 on June 25, 1969. When his wife Clara died on March 17, 1977, the five children assumed the estate. They formed a partnership with Robert Eugene as head partner, and today they jointly operate the diversified Kershaw investments living by the motto taught them by their parents: "Do unto others as you would have them do unto you."

EDWARD PHILLIP KIRSCHNER

Harry Kirschner.

Edward Phillip Kirschner.

Sarah Kirschner.

Although many people in Muskogee do not know the exact date Edward Phillip "Phil" Kerschner came to the city, all who knew him do remember his smile, his friendliness, and his astute business mind.

Phil, born on May 17, 1896, came to northeastern Oklahoma with his parents, Harry and Sarah Kirschner, in the early 1900s. They settled in Haskell, later moving to Muskogee. Phil graduated from Central High School and then joined his father in the mercantile and oil business, but by 1918 their investments in petroleum had become so large they sold their store and devoted all their time and energy to oil.

It was in oil that Phil Kirschner rose to prominence. He never attended college, believing that practical experience was the best teacher and the world the best school. Mostly by experience in the field, he learned the oil business so well that geologists visited him for consultation, and he studied and learned all aspects of the business world. Once a year Phil wrote an investment letter to a few close friends, but in later years the letter was in such demand and the mailing list of such huge proportions that, because of failing health, he had to discontinue it.

Phil had interests in oil and land throughout Oklahoma, as well as in Kansas, Texas, and Canada. According to Roberta, his wife since July 23, 1954, many of Phil's investments were in oil leases purchased on Indian land. He always respected and appreciated the Indians because of his "luck," as Roberta calls it, on their land. The Creek Nation in turn showed its appreciation for him by declaring "Phil Kirschner Days" on May 27 and June 3, 1981.

Although Phil was widely traveled, learning and sharing as he traveled, he always returned to and was happiest in his favorite classroom—Muskogee and the Oklahoma oil fields. Throughout his career, which made him one of Oklahoma's most trusted and respected businessmen, he shared generously with others as his material wealth increased. He donated large amounts to the Boy Scouts of America and Goodwill Industries, and he set up numerous scholarships for orphans and the handicapped. He also gave money and equipment to the Albert Einstein College of Medicine and Yeshiva University in New York. At his own expense he brought Rabbis and other Jewish religious leaders to Muskogee from Tulsa and Oklahoma City in order that a sufficient number of Jewish males would be present for services as specified in Jewish law.

Phil established a tradition— and provided in his will so that this tradition would be continued—of presenting silver candle sticks to any Jewish girl who could recite the Ten Commandments in both Hebrew and English. A silver Kiddush Cup is given to any Jewish boy who can perform the same task. He also made donations to church denominations outside his own faith.

He was a member of the Muskogee Chamber of Commerce, the Shriners, and other civic organizations. He donated and equipped playgrounds and tennis courts for the benefit of Muskogee youth. And he bought 10 acres of land, donated it to the Azalea Park, and gave the fountain in the center of the park as a memorial to his parents.

Often he spoke to students in area schools about his belief in America and "Americanism," always encouraging young people to take advantage of the opportunity here.

It is not important that some people do not remember when Phil, son of a Polish immigrant who fled Europe to escape persecution, came to Muskogee. What is important is that Muskogee remembers a man with a business mind almost unequaled and a man who loved his fellow man and his community. With his death on May 2, 1981, Muskogee lost a citizen who will never be forgotten and who can never be replaced in the hearts of those who knew and loved him.

LEAKE INDUSTRIES, INC.

James C. Leake is indeed a true Oklahoma pioneer. He was born and raised on a farm at Chandler, Oklahoma, homesteaded by his grandfather in the Sac and Fox Land Run of 1891. His grandfather had come to America from England and had homesteaded in Guthrie in the first Oklahoma land run of 1889 and was working as a law clerk in Guthrie when the Sac and Fox and Pottawatomie lands were first laid out for future settlement. Using the information he gained in the clerk's office, he paid $1 for a ride to within six miles of the planned township site of Chandler, then walked the remaining distance. At daybreak the following morning he walked two and one-half miles east of Chandler and homesteaded the 160-acre farm that is still owned by the family today.

James C. Leake, as many other Oklahomans, grew up in a rural society and lived through the depression years on a farm. In spite of hardships—and by holding a succession of jobs, such as a dry cleaning broker and processor, in a flower shop, and at a Safeway Grocery Company—Leake worked his way through the University of Oklahoma.

It was while attending college that he met Marjory Griffin, who became his wife. Marjory was the daughter of J. T. Griffin and sister of John T. Griffin. James and Marjory were married on September 10, 1940, and have resided in Muskogee since 1945.

In partnership with his brother-in-law John T. Griffin, the two families set about forging one of the great companies in Oklahoma history. The nucleus, of course, was the Griffin Grocery Company,

James C. Leake.

founded by J. T. Griffin in 1908. Using the grocery company as the strong nucleus and expanding radio interests J. T. Griffin had acquired prior to World War II, John Griffin and James C. Leake expanded into television. On December 19, 1953, KATV in Little Rock, Arkansas, went on the air, followed by KWTV in Oklahoma City the following day. KTUL, Channel 8, first located in Mus-

kogee, began broadcasting on September 18, 1954. From this initial foray into broadcasting, the stations have prospered, and today they are among the leading affiliates in the United States.

In 1969 the Griffins and Leakes dissolved their partnership. The old Griffin-Leake Television, Inc., became Century Communications with John Griffin taking Channel 9 in Oklahoma City and the grocery company. The Leakes took Channel 7 in Little Rock and Channel 8 in Tulsa.

185

In addition to these interests, the Leake family now holds a license to construct a station near San Juan, Puerto Rico, and numerous other business opportunities.

Despite his heavy schedule of work, Leake has found time to serve in various positions in Oklahoma. He is a member of the Oklahoma Hall of Fame, as is his brother-in-law John T. Griffin. He has served on countless committees, boards, and state functions.

City and County Port Authority. In this latter position, he has been instrumental in securing several large industries for the Muskogee area and has become a recognized expert in the field of inland port management.

Perhaps one of the things for which Leake is most noted is his lifelong love of things mechanical. The Leake family enjoys one of the most prestigious old car collections in the world. Leake is a rec-

world. He has taken part in numerous old car international events. During one of these events, his cars were reviewed by and he personally met the Queen of England.

The Leakes have four children: Jim Leake, Jr., the oldest; John C. Leake; and two daughters, Jean and Nancy. All the children are active in the family business and were educated through high school in Muskogee.

Marjory and James Leake with J. Paul Getty (seated) at his castle in England.

He is past Chairman of the Will Rogers Commission and has served on the Governor's Southern Growth Policies Committee, and as director of different banks. Currently he is a director of the First National Bank of Tulsa.

Leake is a recognized leader across the nation not only in the broadcast media, in which he and John T. Griffin both are pioneers, but also in tourism and promotion, in the areas of balanced state growth, public financing, and, unlikely enough, in port management as Chairman of the Muskogee

ognized authority on Rolls-Royces and Bentleys and maintains one of the finest private collections in existence. His lifelong hobby has turned into a marvelous museum located in Muskogee where local residents and tourists alike may enjoy his unparalleled collections of antique cars. Leake's Antique Car Auction, held each year in June, draws participants from around the

James C. Leake truly exemplifies the spirit and determination of Oklahomans. Where else but in America, particularly in Oklahoma, could early-day pioneers like J. T. Griffin and his children, John and Marjory, and James C. Leake have come from such humble beginnings to the achievements and success they now enjoy. This is a tribute to the American way of life and to the perseverance of individuals.

MADEWELL METAL CORPORATION

The city of Muskogee was founded by pioneer families who believed that a little luck, a lot of hard work, and prayer would bring success. The same holds true today. Madewell Metal Corporation, at 301 West Shawnee, is a perfect example of this.

Elmo Madewell is no stranger to work. Born on October 19, 1924, in Muskogee and educated in local schools, he worked with his father throughout his adolescent years. After graduating from high school, he took a job with Broadway Theaters, Inc., and on February 7, 1942, he married Ruby Curtis of Muskogee. One year later he left Broadway Theaters to enter the ministry.

Two years after his marriage, Elmo in 1944, at age 20, built the first Church of God house of worship in Muskogee at B and Cincinnati streets. He served as State Youth Director in Oklahoma for the Churches of God in 1948 and 1949. This church in Muskogee was not to be the last "first" church Elmo would build. He also built the first Church of God building in Mexico and a church in the Philippine Islands in the early 1960s. And during the mid-1960s he built churches in Indonesia, Alaska, and throughout Oklahoma. In the early 1970s he was instrumental in building a Church of God orphanage in Brazil.

Although these accomplishments would seem a full life's work for most people, they are only part of what Elmo accomplished. In 1950 he bought five acres of land on West Shawnee on which was located one rickety building. After acquiring the land, Elmo went to a local bank to

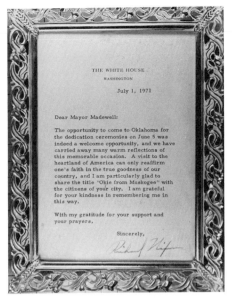

Above: President Nixon's letter to Mayor Madewell. Below: The truck with which Elmo Madewell started his business.

borrow money to purchase his first piece of equipment for his newly organized Madewell Metal Corporation—$2100 for a 1950 Chevrolet pick up truck. Elmo was the sole employee of the firm.

Today that 1950 pick up has been replaced by some 45 specially designed and built tractor-trailer units. These trucks travel across 15 states to pick up scrap metal and old batteries for recycling at Madewell. And that one original employee has grown to a work force of 45 to 50, including the Madewell truck drivers. There now are

five buildings at the Muskogee plant and, since 1975, a branch plant in Tulsa on North Lewis. The Tulsa plant recycles scrap metal, while the Muskogee plant salvages lead from old batteries.

Meanwhile, as Elmo gave much of his time and energy to his evangelistic work in addition to Madewell Metal, he still somehow found time to become politically involved in the community. From 1970 to 1972 he served as mayor of Muskogee, during which time he instituted the city's "Okie from Muskogee" program, a promotional effort that stressed pride in having a Muskogee heritage. Some of the recipients of these certificates were Merle Haggard (who began the program thanks to his recording, "Okie From Muskogee"), James Whitmore (for his portrayal of Will Rogers), several of the original astronauts, T. G. Shepherd, and many others, but the one which meant the most to Elmo was the certificate he presented President Richard M. Nixon. In return he received a hand-signed note from the President expressing pride in being an "Okie from Muskogee"; this Elmo prizes greatly.

Today, although Elmo remains president of Madewell Metal Corporation, he devotes most of his time to what he considers his true purpose in life, his mission and evangelistic work, because his two sons and his son-in-law have taken over most of the day-to-day operations of Madewell Metal. Elmo's oldest son David is vice president, Don is secretary-treasurer, and Steve Allred is plant manager in Tulsa.

MANHATTAN CONSTRUCTION COMPANY

Two Manhattan projects: Camp Gruber (left) and Convention Hall in Guthrie (right).

On November 16, 1907, Oklahoma became the 46th state in the Union, and Manhattan Construction Company applied for a corporate charter under Oklahoma law. One month and one day later it became the first firm to be incorporated by the new state, and thus with Oklahoma celebrates its 75th birthday in 1982.

The company was founded by Laurence H. Rooney, who was born in Iowa on January 1, 1860, and came to Oklahoma in 1895. He operated a general store in Chandler and did construction contracting on the side until 1906 when his sideline had grown to such an extent that he and L. D. Lewman incorporated under the laws of New York because Oklahoma at that time was not a state. The company and its founder moved to Muskogee in 1910.

Manhattan's first big contract was for the construction of the state capitol at Guthrie. The building had to be completed in three months for the first session of the legislature. The deadline was met.

A few notable Manhattan projects during this early period were: Muskogee General Hospital, 1922; Perrine Building, Oklahoma City, 1926; First National Bank, Oklahoma City, 1931; Phillips Petroleum, 1933; International Harvester, 1937; the original Tulsa Union Depot, 1920; and current restoration

of that building now underway.

Laurence F. Rooney, L. H.'s son born in 1895, began full-time work for Manhattan in 1914. He assumed direction of the company in 1937 when his father died.

During World War II Manhattan constructed Camps Gruber and Chaffee, the Douglas Plant in Tulsa, and numerous other government facilities across the nation. Through this period the company had a peak employment of 80,000. The constructing of Camp Gruber in four months was hailed as one of the outstanding civilian construction jobs of World War II, and after completing Camp Chaffee in the same length of time Manhattan was awarded the Army-Navy "E" Award for excellence.

In 1943 Manhattan began its first project for American Airlines. The Oklahoma A & M Library was built in 1948, the University of Oklahoma Student Union in 1949, and the First National Bank of Tulsa in 1950. The 12-floor Adams Building in Bartlesville, the Boeing hangers in Wichita, Kansas (which were the largest overhead door assemblies in the world at that time), and the First National Bank of Oklahoma City all were completed in the late 1950s.

L. F. Rooney, Jr., began working for the company in 1947, and after a series of varying responsibilities, including three years in

Houston with Manhattan of Texas and field supervision over the University of Oklahoma Student Union building, he became President in 1960. In addition to guiding the continued growth of the company, Mr. Rooney, like his father, was deeply involved in the Associated General Contractors, both at state and national levels. He served as President of the Oklahoma Chapter in 1961 and 1962, and as the organization's national President during 1978.

The 1960s and 1970s have witnessed some of Manhattan's most impressive projects, including the Texas Medical Center in Houston, the 50-story First National Tower in Tulsa, the Tulsa Assembly Center, the Ford Glass Plant in Tulsa, St. John's Hospital, Oral Roberts University, and many others.

Manhattan also constructed the terminals at the Dallas-Fort Worth International Airport, Will Rogers World Airport in Oklahoma City, and others.

Manhattan was ranked the 20th largest general building contractor in the United States by the *Engineering News-Record* for 1980, and has been responsible for the construction of more than 50 percent of the court houses in Oklahoma.

For more than 75 years, Manhattan has been building a tradition of excellence in construction and will continue that tradition in the future.

MUSKOGEE GENERAL HOSPITAL

The first city-owned and operated hospital, the forerunner of today's Muskogee General Hospital began under the name Physicians and Surgeons Hospital in 1911 on South Border. However, within a few years the city had outgrown the hospital, and it was relocated on Agency Hill in Honor Heights (at the site of the present Veterans Administration Hospital). It occupied these facilities from 1922 to 1926.

Population growth and the need for a more central location mandated a change, and the hospital bought and renovated the old Spaulding Institute building on Baltimore and Okmulgee. Formal open house ceremonies were held in 1928.

That same year Edna Rockefeller, R.N., came to visit Muskogee and offered to help prepare for the opening of a new Muskogee General Hospital. This was the beginning of an affiliation that would span 40 years and include her duties as Administrator, Surgical Supervisor, Director of Nursing Services, Director of the hospital's School of Nursing, and Director of Volunteer Services. "Miss Rocky," as she affectionately was known throughout the community, retired from Muskogee General in 1968 and died in the hospital 10 years later.

During World War II a dormitory for nurses was added. The building on Baltimore and Okmulgee gradually became outdated, however, and in 1959 land was purchased and construction begun on new facilities at 300 Rockefeller Drive, the hospital's present location. The new structure, with 110 beds, opened on April 8, 1959.

Since that time the hospital has undergone four major expansions. From 110 beds it grew to 175

Members of the Muskogee General Hospital School of Nursing, Class of 1951, present a class gift to Earl Benson, hospital administrator, in front of the original Muskogee General building on Baltimore and Okmulgee.

in 1960, to 225 in 1964, to 275 in 1969; the fourth expansion, completed in 1977, doubled the square footage and increased the number of beds to 366.

Except for the original 110-bed facility, the entire hospital properties have been developed through the sale of revenue trust bonds to private investors and assistance from Hill-Burton (federal) grant monies. All investor funds are repaid entirely through charges for services rendered to patients using the facility. Muskogee General receives no federal, state, or local tax support.

However, strong support from the community is provided by the Muskogee General Hospital Aux-

iliary and the Volunteer Service. The Auxiliary was founded in 1950 by Elizabeth Anthis "to give voluntary assistance to the hospital," and since then has contributed generously in money and service.

The Volunteer Service, a functional department at Muskogee General, presently consists of 350 men, women, and teen-agers representing the community who give of their time to be of service to hospital patients and visitors.

Today's $30 million facility indeed is a regional medical center currently incorporating some of the most modern technology available to support the medical needs of northeastern Oklahoma.

Muskogee General Hospital today.

RICKETTS ENTERPRISES

William H. Ricketts, who was born, raised, and educated (with the exception of four years at Oklahoma State University) in Muskogee, returned to the city in 1967 with one purpose in mind—to retain in or return to Muskogee the talent and opportunity which had left due to the city's non-growth.

Before his return, Bill had started and operated an engineering company in Stillwater between 1965 and 1967. When he and his family returned to Muskogee, Bill freely admits times were lean until the founding of Ricketts Construction in the spring of 1972—with himself and one secretary comprising the entire work force.

The young company enjoyed immediate success. In November of 1972 A. J. Roth joined the firm as general manager and superintendent of construction. In 1975 Three Rivers Steel of Muskogee was established, and that same year Gary Kutz joined the company as chief estimator. The next year William F. Scrimminger became the president of the newest Ricketts' enterprise, the Muskogee Environmental Conservation Company. Shortly afterward, Curt Freeling and Terry Groom became a part of the growing Ricketts' organization as vice president and estimator, respectively, of the construction company.

In 1977 Stephen A. Crank, one of Bill's lifelong friends, who also had attended Oklahoma State University, became a stockholder in the corporation as well as executive vice president and general manager of Three Rivers Steel. He joined Bill and A. J. in their efforts to provide jobs and opportunity for the youth of Muskogee. This they accomplish in several ways: by taking young men and women into the company and helping them become established, and by supporting area schools both academ-

Phoenix S & L, a Rickett's building.

ically and athletically. Both personal and company scholarships are made available to outstanding high school seniors, and generous donations are given for athletic needs.

Bill's most recent (and perhaps most important undertaking to date) is a package plan involving Ricketts Enterprises and other firms in the restoration of the old Severs Hotel building. One of the first brick structures constructed in Muskogee, the Severs is a symbol of the growth and opportunity in Muskogee's past, and, according to Bill, again will symbolize the growth and opportunity in present and future Muskogee.

And as Bill has become a major force moving Muskogee forward, so also has Ricketts Enterprises progressed. Its work force has grown to 50 full-time employees with, at times, as many as 250 part-time employees.

Ricketts Construction specializes in all phases of construction: commercial, industrial, and residential. Among its accomplish-

ments are the home and branch offices of Phoenix Federal Savings and Loan, City Bank, the Egan plant, and three plants for Zapata Industries (one in North Carolina, one in California, and the home plant in Muskogee). Ricketts has constructed additions to several area schools, such as at Bacone College, Northeastern State University, Sequoyah High School (in Tahlequah), and the Indian Capital Vo-Tech. The firm also has built numerous custom homes, such as that of James C. Leake.

Three Rivers Steel manufactures to specifications steel bridge girders, steel used in the construction of commercial and industrial buildings, industrial heaters, and oil drilling rigs.

Although Bill has made many major contributions to Muskogee, his largest commitment by far is to the youth of Muskogee and the future growth and development of the city itself. Ricketts Enterprises is proud of Muskogee's past and confident of its future.

The H. B. Egan Manufacturing plant, constructed by Ricketts.

190

ROWSEY MEMORIAL CHAPEL

The Rowsey Memorial Chapel, a gift from Paul E. Rowsey, Sr., W. E. Rowsey, Jr., and Mrs. William Eugene Rowsey in memory of William Eugene Rowsey, was dedicated on Sunday, April 3, 1960.

W. E. Rowsey was one of the organizers and founders of St. Paul Methodist Church, a charter member, the first chairman of the Board of Stewards, and served on the Board from the time the church was organized until his death on July 23, 1954. He also served as chairman of the Music Committee for many years and sang tenor in the church choir.

Before coming to Muskogee, Mr. Rowsey, who was born in Henderson, Tennessee, had been principal of a school, a college president, and Clerk of the Federal Court at Miami. He and several friends organized the first bank in Miami, and he was Chief Executive Officer of that institution until 1901 when he resigned to come to Muskogee.

Mr. Rowsey continued his association with different banks in Muskogee and other towns. At one time he either was president or vice president of five separate banks. He was organizer and director of the original Muskogee Chamber of Commerce and acted as secretary without salary for its first year.

W. E. Rowsey, Jr., with the support of the Rowsey family, was responsible for the arrangements necessary for building the Rowsey Memorial Chapel in memory of a man who was truly one of Mus-

Above: W. E. Rowsey.

kogee's founding fathers.

In addition to the building itself, the chapel was completely furnished by the Rowsey family, including the pews, organ, altar, and pulpit furnishings. The nave seats 100 persons, and 20 may be seated in the Chancel area. The chapel is used for weddings, Holy Communion Services, private meditations, prayer, baptisms, and other special services for small groups.

One of the more interesting features of the chapel is the skylight arrangement which floods the altar with sunlight on clear days. The 35 foot spire—pointing toward the sky, lifting a crown upward—is a reminder of the King of Kings, Jesus Christ.

The chapel is of cream, buff, and gray sandstone from Tennessee and blends with the Mother Church, St. Paul United Methodist Church, which stands in the same block at 21st Street and West Okmulgee. The stained glass in the chapel was hand blown in Germany. The marble in the altar was imported from Italy. The large, laminated fir master rafters came from the state of Washington. The slate in the floor was shipped from Vermont. The figure of Christ at the front of the chapel was sculpted at Denton, Texas. The chapel, reflecting a Gothic and modern theme throughout, has a total floor space of 2000 square feet.

Rowsey Memorial Chapel was designed by J. Murrell Bennett of the Bennett and Crittenden Architectural Firm in Dallas.

Following in the Rowsey family tradition, Paul E. Rowsey, Sr., who died on June 8, 1971, stipulated in his will a bequest to continue the work of St. Paul United Methodist Church.

ST. PAUL UNITED METHODIST CHURCH

St. Paul United Methodist Church was established as the Methodist Episcopal Church South in September of 1878 with three members, an unfinished building on the corner of Cherokee Street and Okmulgee Avenue, unlimited faith, and a prayer.

By 1886 the building (the old Rock Church) was finished, a parsonage had been built, and church membership had increased to 162. In 1904 a fire destroyed the church building but not the spirit of its congregation. They simply changed their place of worship to the Spaulding College Chapel (Harrell Institute), and later to Gavigan Hall, a local dance hall. Wednesday night prayer meetings were held in the First Presbyterian Church.

That same year the church membership divided, one part naming itself the First Methodist Church and serving a congregation on the east side of the MK&T railroad, and the other part, later to become St. Paul, serving those on the west side of the railroad. The Reverend E. M. Sweet was the first pastor of St. Paul.

In 1905 the church acquired its own building, which was moved to the southwest corner of Fourth and Wall streets. On December 4 that year the cornerstone was laid

for a new church at a new location: Division (Seventh) Street and Boston. The congregation worshipped in the new church on December 30, 1906,

On January 27, 1929, disaster struck again, a fire that destroyed the church building. Following this conflagration, services were held in the Masonic Temple while the determined members rebuilt their house of worship. First services were held in the Social Hall of the church at its new location at 23rd and West Okmulgee on July 12, 1931, and in the completed sanctuary on April 25, 1932. The name of the church was changed to St. Paul Methodist Church in 1929.

In the mid-1940s the church, debt free, was dedicated, and the Griffin memorial organ, a gift from J. T. Griffin in memory of his wife, Ada Toole Griffin, was installed. Church membership had reached 840. The church chimes, a gift from Jere Lock in memory of his parents, chimed for the first time in 1946. A total of $8000 was pledged by St. Paul and its congregation in 1948 to help Ridgecrest Methodist Church become organized.

St. Paul gave its first broadcast on KMUS radio in June of 1947. The Rowsey Memorial Chapel, funded and furnished by the Rowsey family in memory of William Eugene Rowsey, was dedicated in April of

1960. A new lending library was started in 1953 as well as a new radio program, "Sunday School of the Air." That same year church membership reached 2200. In 1956 another milestone was reached when Sam Slack, the first missionary from St. Paul's, was sent into the field.

A master plan for continued expansion was presented to and accepted by the official church board in 1957. A year later a weekday nursery began, and the sanctuary, with a seating capacity that had reached 500, was redecorated.

Ground breaking ceremonies for a new educational building were held in April of 1961, and the building, with 18 classrooms, was consecrated in 1962. A new parsonage was purchased in December 1963, and 10 years later a second parsonage was secured for the assistant pastor. A recreation room also was added in the 1960s.

St. Paul United Methodist Church, which will celebrate its 80th anniversary in 1983, has a continuing expansion program that will reach years into the future. As Muskogee and its spiritual needs grow, so will St. Paul United Methodist Church continue to grow in order to serve the community in the spirit of Christ.

SERVICE LEAGUE OF MUSKOGEE

In 1935 Mrs. Howell Parks, local Red Cross director, asked a group of young women to help with the clerical work in her office. From this group, Service League of Muskogee was founded. In 1937 Jo Ballentine was elected first president of the 17-member League.

Early services provided by this all-volunteer group included Red Cross and County Health Unit work, providing games and music for the Day Nursery, assisting with Girl Scout and YWCA camps, distributing baskets to the needy, and transcribing books into Braille for the School for the Blind.

The war years were busy for the League. Gifts for the wounded were wrapped, nursing duties were performed, and fund-raising benefits were held. Membership, which in 1940 stood at 24, reached 35 in 1946.

The League emphasized fund-raising projects in the late 1940s and early 1950s. A 10-year run of rummage sales was initiated, and the League assisted in the restoration of the Indian Agency Building. Facilities at the Murrow Indian Orphanage at Bacone College were improved with money raised by the League. Eye glasses were bought, and two eye operations for children were paid for. Leaguers led the Heart and Polio fund drives and staffed the Blood Bank. Donations were made to the YWCA and to Muskogee General Hospital.

Applications were made by the League to become affiliated with the Association of Junior Leagues of America in 1959-1960, but the application was denied. Provisional courses were initiated in 1960, and contributions were made to the Baptist Hospital, the Museum project, the Day Care Nursery, and Muskogee's Public Library in 1962 and 1963. The following year a pledge of $6000 was made to the Museum payable over a three-year period. That pledge was paid in full in 1966. During the last half of the 1960s, almost $15,000 was raised and donated to various organizations by the Leaguers. And even with all this work, the Leaguers still found time to assist with the testing of all grade school children in Muskogee for learning disabilities.

The decade of the 1970s brought increased fund-raising efforts and membership. Old projects were refunded and repledged. New projects were added—milk for underpriviliged children, a bike trail, a typewriter for the museum, camp funds for the Salvation Army, assistance to the Azalea Gardens— the list is endless, and services in the 1980s promise to be even greater.

One major step already has been taken. In May of 1982 four $500 scholarships were given to area high school seniors. These seniors were judged by a committee on academic performance and need. In the fall of 1980 and the fall of 1981, Monte Carlo Fund Projects have raised more than $16,000 to benefit Muskogee charities.

All efforts of the 37 members and 12 provisionals of the Service League are directed to service to the community. All work is voluntary, and, although the early history of the Service League is hazy and unclear, the accomplishments, dedication, and support to the Muskogee community by this group of women is very bright and definite.

Outgoing 1981-1982 officers are: Sally Beckman, President; Kathy Allred, Vice President; Lynn Thornley, Treasurer; Chrissie Wagner, Recording Secretary; and Kay Jones, Corresponding Secretary.

New 1982-1983 officers include: Kathy Allred, President; Mickey Madewell, Vice President; Marilyn Gilder, Treasurer; Marilyn Roth, Recording Secretary; and Shawn Dickman, Corresponding Secretary.

WARNER-BORUM-WARNER RANCH

The Warner-Borum-Warner Ranch, 14 miles southwest of Muskogee, is the oldest ranch under continuous ownership in northeastern Oklahoma. The 9500-acre, crescent-shaped spread, stocked with approximately 2000 head of registered and commercial Hereford cattle, began as a 160-acre gathering point for grain from small farms in the area. This first acreage was purchased by E. W. Warner and R. C. Borum on May 1, 1909.

E. S. Warner—father of William S. Warner, Sr., and grandfather of William S. Warner, Jr.—moved from Davenport, Iowa, to Muskogee in 1904. He was working as an immigration agent for the Frisco Railroad. R. C. Borum moved to Muskogee from Winchester, Illinois, in 1905, and began working as Warner's accountant in 1906. After a strong friendship developed, a partnership was formed.

By 1909, E. W. Warner, operating a land and trust company, was managing all the city investments, while R. C. Borum was overseeing the company's farm holdings. The same family arrangement holds today. More land was added to the ranch in 1910; then in 1965 came the purchase of "The Old Stebbins Ranch," which brought the ranch to its present size.

During the early years, cattle ranching was a sideline. During the Teens, they raised wheat, corn, and cotton, the few cattle on the ranch acquired through default on notes. By the early 1920s wheat prices had dropped so low that the partners began reseeding the land in Bermuda grass and turning it back to grazing land. During this period a continuing program of soil and water conservation began. The Pecan watershed on the ranch was the first Soil Conservation Service Water Shed in northeastern Oklahoma. Every type of soil and water improvement was undertaken. The ranch also would later become the first in Oklahoma to inoculate its entire herd against Brucelosis (Bangs) disease.

In the late 1920s the decision was made to change completely to raising Hereford cattle. Until this time, according to Richard Borum, there had been only "cows and even a few hogs" on the ranch. By the late 1950s everything on the ranch was Hereford. The main sire herd now in use is made up of Onward, Evan Mischief, and English-bred bulls introduced into the herd in the late 1960s. The cow herd, both registered and commercial, is basically Onward.

Until 1936, when Albert Borum and his family moved to the ranch, all the owners had lived in Muskogee. Richard and his family moved to the ranch in 1940 to oversee the pastures and feed. Albert manages the cattle.

During the early 1930s most of the cattle were commercial, but toward the end of the decade the partners began leaning more toward registered Herefords—five registered to three commercial. After World War II, because of a shortage of help and because it required less paperwork, the ratio of commercial to registered swung the other way—seven to three, the same as today.

In the early years only the commercial herd was branded with the first ranch brand, a triangle. The registered herd was marked on each horn, but after rustling became a problem (and still is to a lesser degree), both herds were branded. The triangle brand has been changed to a more difficult-to-copy Broken Heart brand.

The original partners were E. W. Warner, R. C. Borum, and W. S. Warner, Sr. Today's partnership is Albert B. and Richard C. Borum, W. S. Warner, Sr., and W. S. Warner, Jr.

AMERICAN BANK OF MUSKOGEE

The American Bank of Muskogee, one of the city's youngest banks, was chartered in May of 1970 and was organized with a capital stock of $187,500 and a surplus of $187,500. Total deposits at the end of its first year— December 31, 1970—were $2,315,467.21, with total assets of $2,940,123.95.

The original organizers of American Bank were, for the most part, from areas other than Muskogee with one exception, Robert E. Kershaw, a native of Muskogee.

American Bank did not begin to show real growth until after it was purchased in 1973 by John A. Baker, present President and Chief Executive Officer, and his associates. Mr. Kershaw became Chairman of the Board of Directors.

Although American Bank cannot claim to have contributed a great deal to the past history of Muskogee, due to its young age, it is evident by its progress that it will contribute a great deal to the city's future.

The original American Bank building already has been expanded, and plans for a second addition within the year have been completed.

Twelve years after its opening—in May of 1982—total deposits of American Bank are $41,469,586.25 and total assets are $50,971,932.86. The bank has a total of 31 officers and employees, all active in the community.

Directors of American Bank are: Robert E. Kershaw, Chairman; John A. Baker; James F. Clark; Edward H. Fite, Jr., M.D.; Jerry F. McKay; Athol Sayre; Glenn Smith; and John Stoia.

Officers of the bank are: John A. Baker, President and Chief Executive Officer; Jerry F. McKay, Executive Vice President; James L. Phillips, Vice President; Scott Scherer, Vice President and Cashier; Lolita Elliott, Assistant Vice President; Wanda Lashley, Assistant Vice President; Jim Welch, Assistant Vice President; Mark P. Lemons, Jr., Assistant Vice President; Betty Smythe, Assistant Vice President; Marilyn Holliday, Asistant Cashier; and Raylene Wolfle, Secretary to the Board.

CITY BANK

City Bank opened its doors on July 9, 1973. At that time there were three banks in existence in the downtown Muskogee area, all established for many years, and there was a newly chartered bank on the west side of town.

Approximately four years prior to the opening of City Bank, eight men had seen the need for a new bank on the east side of Muskogee. These men, who later became the incorporators of the bank, were: J. T. Hannah, Chairman; K. C. Love, Jr.; R. Forney Sandlin; W. L. "Bill" Stone; Morris Caves; Coleman Fite; and W. B. Kennedy. These men brought diversified backgrounds to the bank, for their occupations included banking, the

bottling business, the law, real estate investments, manufacturing, farming, and retail clothing. It took four years to obtain a state charter because of the resistance of three of the existing banks.

When City Bank opened in 1973, it was housed in a temporary building 26 x 48 feet plus four drive-

in windows and a complement of 11 officers and employees. It remained in this temporary location for approximately one year and three months while its permanent building was under construction on the same acreage as the temporary location.

The new building is of colonial design and covers 8400 square feet. The balance of the almost three acres provides space for drive-through windows and ample parking for banking customers.

The original capital of the bank was $500,000. This has grown to approximately $3 million with total assets of $33 million. There are 10 officers and 21 employees of City Bank of Muskogee.

FANSTEEL, INC.

Fansteel of Muskogee is one of three metal division plants of Fansteel, Inc., headquartered in North Chicago, Illinois. Fansteel was founded in 1907, incorporated in 1917, and became a subsidiary of H. D. Porter Company, Inc., in 1976.

The Muskogee facility, which, in essence, combines an extraction plant, a reduction plant, and a consolidation plant for the production of tantalum and columbium metals and compounds, began in Muskogee in 1957 with three main buildings—two production plants and one service building. Located on 110 acres on the west bank of the Arkansas River near the Port of Muskogee, the plant has grown to employ 130 persons. Other major buildings have been added through the years, the most recent being the

Research and Development facility, which was completed in 1981.

Tantalum raw materials processed at the Muskogee plant are received from Thailand, Canada, Australia, Brazil, West Germany, and Africa. The major use for tantalum is in an electronic device called a capacitor. A tantalum in-

got, eight inches in diameter and 10 feet long ($2\frac{1}{2}$ times heavier than steel), will weigh approximately 3600 pounds. In June of 1982, tantalum metal sold for $150 to $250 a pound. In addition to tantalum, the Muskogee plant also produces columbium ingot, bar, powder, alloys, oxides, and carbides.

Past managers of the Muskogee Fansteel plant were Lyle Clark, Larry Wise, Gil Isaacson, and Conrad L. Brown who served for 13 years. Jim Pierret, who came to the position in 1977, is the current plant manager.

Pierret has been with Fansteel, Inc., since 1956. He came to Muskogee in 1967 as Plant Technical Director. He and his wife Joan and their six sons, now Muskogee residents for 15 years, consider this city and its people their home and their friends.

FIRST BANK OF HASKELL

The First Bank of Haskell, established in 1904 as the First National Bank of Haskell, moved in 1905 into one of the first brick buildings erected in the town of Haskell. The founding officers were H. P. Hubbard, President; Carr Peterson, Vice President; Cleat Peterson, Cashier; and R. P. Beshara, Assistant Cashier. The bank opened with $25,000 capital stock.

The bank remained in the Peterson family with George M. Floyd as President in later years, and Paul Peterson, son of Cleat Peterson, until 1966 when the bank was purchased by Harold A. French.

During the French ownership, the bank underwent complete remodeling and expansion. Parking facilities and drive-through windows were added, making it the bank it is today. When it became a state bank in the early 1970s, the

name was changed to First Bank of Haskell.

In October of 1981, First Bank again changed owners. The Mabrey family—Carlisle, Jr., and his wife, Lurline—purchased the bank. The Mabreys were born and raised in Okmulgee, where they still re-

side. In addition to First Bank of Haskell, the Mabreys also own the Citizen's National Bank in Okmulgee and other business interests.

Directors of the bank at the time of the sale to the Mabreys were Harold A. French, Verna Marie French, A. B. Bayouth, George L. Sallee, Jr., Delores Sallee, Russel Alberty, and Arthur I. Carter.

Current Directors are Gary Winters, President; John Mabrey, Vice President; Bruce Mabrey; Marilyn Mabrey; Carlisle Mabrey, Jr.; and Carlisle Mabrey, III. John, Carlisle, III, Bruce, and Marilyn are the children of Lurline and Carlisle Mabrey, Jr.

First Bank of Haskell, serving the community of Haskell for 78 years, proud of its heritage, believing in its future, today has assets of more than $9 million.

H.E. KETCHAM LUMBER DEALERS, INC.

The year 1982 is a time of dual celebration for H. E. Ketcham Lumber Dealers, Inc., for not only is the company celebrating Oklahoma's Diamond Jubilee but also its own Diamond Anniversary.

H. E. Ketcham, who moved to Muscogee, Indian Territory, in 1898, opened the first lumber yard on North Mill Street in 1907, and although today the Muskogee retail lumber yard is located at 316 North Main the original location is still used for storage.

Throughout the Teens and Twenties, the company grew until there were 32 Ketcham retail yards located across Oklahoma and Kansas. During the depression years and the late Thirties, however, when many small northeastern Oklahoma towns collapsed economically, Ketcham Lumber closed the doors on all but five of its branches.

At the close of World War II, H.

E.'s son Lee, born September 30, 1921, joined his father in the business. Lee attended local elementary and junior high schools and received his high school diploma from Shattuck Military Academy in Faribault, Minnesota. He attended the University of Oklahoma for two years, but his college career was cut short by the outbreak of World War II.

After joining the company, Lee managed Ketcham Lumber, which was incorporated in 1959, until his death on December 30, 1981. At that time, control and management of the corporation passed to

Lee's two sons—Gary Lee, president and general manager, and Thomas (Tom) Ed, vice president and manager of the Muskogee yard.

Gary Lee, the oldest, attended local schools and the University of Oklahoma. After majoring in business, he joined the Ketcham Corporation. Tom also attended local elementary and junior high schools; then, like his father, he went to Shattuck Military Academy for his high school diploma, after which he earned a degree in business from Northern Arizona University. Tom and his wife Debra have one daughter.

Today the Ketchams have retail lumber yards in Checotah, Nowata, Warner, and Muskogee. All these are basic retail yards, while the fifth, K Wood, at 2914 West Shawnee, in addition to carrying lumber is a complete home center.

SEVERS HOTEL

The Severs Hotel, one of the few remaining landmarks of Muskogee's early history, was completed in August of 1912 at a cost of $325,000. In his article, "Turning Back the Clock," Dub West wrote, "The Severs opened August 31 with all the pomp and ceremony befitting one of the outstanding hotels of the southwest."

The 12-story hotel hosted all major conventions held by various civic organizations, such as the Rotary, Lions, and Kiwanis. A reception for Alice Robertson, when she was elected to Congress, was held at the Severs. In 1928 the Women's Noonday Club had a sign painted, bearing the word "Muskogee," and placed it on the roof of the Severs as an aid to airplane pilots. Many residents still remember the elegant "Officers'

Club" in the basement of the hotel during World War II.

A few of the well-known guests who stayed at the Severs included Helen Keller, Eugene Debs, Lucille Mulhall, J. C. Penney, Will Rogers (several times), Dr. C. I. Schoffield, Sydney Smith, Charles Lindbergh, Lindbergh's mother, Vice President Charles Curtis, Betty Davis, Tom Mix, and hundreds more.

Captain F. B. Severs, an outstanding pioneer and town builder of Indian Territory, for whom the hotel was named, came to the Three Forks area at age 17. He worked as a clerk in a store, as a school teacher, and was the only white man in the all-Creek regiment during the Civil War. For this, he later was adopted into the tribe. After the Civil War he operated extensive ranching and farming interests in Muskogee and Okmulgee counties, and would become one of Muskogee's leading citizens.

The Severs Hotel, built by a man who believed in Muskogee's future, has had a glorious past. If current restoration plans for the Severs Hotel are completed, this once-elegant building again will be an important part of downtown Muskogee.

SUGGESTED READINGS

Agnew, Brad. *Fort Gibson: Terminal on the Trail of Tears.* Norman: University of Oklahoma Press, 1980.

Benedict, John D. *History of Muskogee and Northeastern Oklahoma.* 3 vols. Chicago: S. J. Clarke Publishing Company, 1922.

Boydstun, Q. B. "The Restoration of Old Fort Gibson." *Chronicles of Oklahoma,* LVIII (Summer 1980), 176-191.

Crockett, Norman L. *The Black Towns.* Lawrence: The Regents Press of Kansas, 1979.

Dawson, Edgar V. "Growth of Education in Muskogee County." Master of Science Thesis, Oklahoma A & M College, 1939.

Debo, Angie. *The Road to Disappearance: A History of the Creek Indians.* Norman: University of Oklahoma Press, 1941.

Faulk, Odie B. *A Full-Service Banker: The Life of Louis W. Duncan.* Oklahoma City: Western Heritage Books, 1981.

_____. *A Man of Vision: The Life and Career of O. W. Coburn.* Oklahoma City: Western Heritage Books, 1980.

Foreman, Carolyn Thomas. "Early History of Webbers Falls." *Chronicles of Oklahoma,* XXIX (Winter 1951-52), 44-483.

Foreman, Grant. *The Five Civilized Tribes.* Norman: University of Oklahoma Press, 1934.

_____. *Indian Removal: The Emigration of the Five Civilized Tribes of Indians.* Norman: University of Oklahoma Press, 1932.

_____. *Muskogee and Eastern Oklahoma.* Muskogee: Muskogee Chamber of Commerce, n.d.

_____. *Muskogee: The Biography of an Oklahoma Town.* Norman: University of Oklahoma Press, 1943.

Fort Gibson Historic Preservtion and Landmark Commission. *Historic Fort Gibson.* N.p., 1982.

Franks, Kenny A. *Stand Watie and the Agony of the Cherokee Nation.* Memphis: Memphis State University Press, 1979.

Gideon, D. C. *History of Indian Territory.* New York: Lewis Publishing Company, 1901.

Irving, Washington. *A Tour on the Prairie.* Norman: University of Oklahoma Press, 1956.

Latrobe, Charles Joseph. *The Rambler in Oklahoma.* Ed. by Muriel H. Wright and George H. Shirk. Oklahoma City: Harlow Publishing Company, 1955.

Marshall, Don A. "Type-of-Farming Development in McIntosh, Muskogee and Warner Counties, Oklahoma. Master of Science Thesis, Oklahoma A & M College, 1938.

Masterson, V. V. *The Katy Railroad and the Last Frontier.* Norman: University of Oklahoma Press, 1978.

Morris, John W., and Edwin C. McReynolds. *Historical Atlas of Oklahoma.* Norman: University of Oklahoma Press, 1965.

Morrison, Daryl. "Twin Territories and Ora Eddleman Reed, Editor," mss. to be published in forthcoming issue of *Chronicles of Oklahoma.*

Muskogee Chamber of Commerce. Assorted pamphlets. *Muskogee, Indian Territory: The Industrial Prodigy of the New Southwest.* Muskogee: John H. N. Tindall Company and the Muskogee Chamber of Commerce, 1906.

Wardell, Morris L. *A Political History of the Cherokee Nation, 1838-1907.* Norman: University of Oklahoma Press, 1938.

West, C. W. "Dub." *Fort Gibson: Gateway to the West.* Muskogee: Muskogee Publishing Company, 1974.

_____ *Muskogee: From Statehood to Pearl Harbor.* Muskogee: Muskogee Publishing Company, 1976.

_____. *Muskogee, I. T.: Queen City of the Southwest.* Muskogee: Muskogee Publishing Company, 1972.

_____. *Persons and Places of Indian Territory.* Muskogee: Muskogee Publishing Company, 1974.

Westbrook, Harriette Johnson. "The Chouteaus and their Commercial Enterprises." *Chronicles of Oklahoma,* XI (June and September 1933), 786-797, 942-966.

Wilson, Charles W., Jr. *Geology of the Muskogee-Porum District, Muskogee and McIntosh Counties, Oklahoma.* Norman: Oklahoma Geological Survey, 1937.

Woodward, Grace Steele. *The Cherokees.* Norman: University of Oklahoma Press, 1963.

ACKNOWLEDGMENTS

In every organization there is one person who can be called upon "to get things done," who is willing to devote long hours of hard work to any worthwhile project. Muskogee and the Five Civilized Tribes Museum are fortunate to have such a person, Martha Watson Griffin. She and her husband John have given many volunteer hours to almost every worthwhile effort in Muskogee, as well as in the state of Oklahoma. When this illustrated history of Muskogee County first was discussed, Martha Watson Griffin was the one who set out to turn dream into reality and who persevered until it happened. To her goes much of the credit for the success of this project.

Assisting her were the members of the Museum's Projects Committee, which consisted of: Mr. Don Bankston, Mrs. Marguerite Bankston, Mr. Richard Bradely, Maxeene Bridwell, Mrs. Frances Rosser Brown, Mrs. R. P. Campbell, Mrs. L.N. Childers, Mrs. Joel Cousins, Mr. Joel Cousins, Mrs. Spencer Denton, Miss Helen Lee Foster, Mrs. L.F. Rooney, Jr., Mrs. James Rowsey, Mrs. Paul Rowsey, Jr., and Miss Gloria Schumann.

Others making the book possible are: Mrs. Cathy Allred, Mrs. Sally Beckman, Mr. and Mrs. William Beckman, Mr. and Mrs. David Carson, Dr. Dwight Darrah, Dorothy Severs English, Fort Gibson State Bank, Mr. and Mrs. K.C. Love, Mrs. Dena Nowotny, and Dr. David Watson.

Foremost among those who helped with the text was C. W. "Dub" West, who for years has researched and written about Muskogee and vicinity. He, along with Frances Rosser Brown and Mrs. George (Marie) Wadley, Jr., read the manuscript carefully for factual content, corrected numerous errors of omission and commission, and rendered invaluable insights.

Equally generous was Troy Anderson, an artist of extraordinary talent who contributed the cover art. Of Cherokee descent, he uses a traditional technique to create paintings that reflect a style of contemporary realism. Rich colors, strong patterns, and expressive figures combine to portray the great pride, the emotion, the spirit, and the reverence for life that are inherent in the American Indian. Not only have his paintings been accepted at numerous one-man and gallery shows across the country, but also his list of honors and awards attest to his popularity and ability.

In this endeavor I also was assisted by Dr. Bob L. Blackburn of the Oklahoma Historical Society, who researched facts and who made helpful suggestions. Dr. Paul F. Lambert spent many hours copying the historic photographs, and Jim Fowler of Muskogee worked hard to make certain the color photography was exactly right, while Jim Argo of Oklahoma City generously contributed the photographs of the Azalea Festival. Others to whom I extend my special gratitude include all those Muskogeeans who allowed their photographs to be copied so that the book would not reprint pictures already seen many times.

Finally I thank Northeastern State University, particularly President Roger Webb, for creating an atmosphere of creative scholarship among the faculty. Thanks to generous support from this institution, I was able to undertake this effort.

In 1910 the Muskogee Free Fair featured a balloon race from Muskogee to St. Louis, Missouri. A photographer caught the start of this exciting event. Courtesy Herman Bresser.

INDEX

The text of this book was set in 11 point Palatino leaded two points. Chapter heads are in 24 point Bookman Demi.

The text paper is 80 pound enamel, patina finish, the cloth Holliston Buckram, with gold leaf stamping. The dust jacket is on 100 pound enamel stock, printed four colors plus varnish.

Composition for the book was furnished by Central Typesetting Company of Memphis and Executive Type of Oklahoma City. Printing and binding were by Rose Printing Company, Tallahassee, Florida.

Project Director: Martha Watson Griffin
Project Editor: James H. Thomas
Design: Bill Williams
Art Production: Steve Posey
Photos: Paul F. Lambert, Jim Fowler, and
   Jim Argo.